Research in Practice

**Dartington Social Research Series**

# Research in Practice

EXPERIMENTS IN DEVELOPMENT AND INFORMATION DESIGN

Roger Bullock
Daniel Gooch
Michael Little
Kevin Mount
*Dartington Social Research Unit*

**Ashgate**
Aldershot • Brookfield USA • Singapore • Sydney

Published by
Ashgate Publishing Limited
Gower House
Croft Road
Aldershot
Hants GU11 3HR
England

Ashgate Publishing Company
Old Post Road
Brookfield
Vermont 05036
USA

**British Library Cataloguing in Publication Data**
Research in practice : experiments in development and
    information design. - (Dartington social research series)
    1.Dartington Social Research Unit 2.Social sciences -
    Research
    I.Bullock, Roger
    300.7'2

**Library of Congress Catalog Card Number:** 98-70908

Printed in the United Kingdom at the University Press, Cambridge

ISBN 1 84014 459 9

# Contents

# Acknowledgements

This book has been prepared by members of the Dartington Social Research Unit, Roger Bullock, Daniel Gooch, Michael Little and Kevin Mount. The work it reports would not have been possible without the considerable sacrifices and effort made by professionals and managers in the nine local authorities that helped with the testing of the *Going Home* materials. In order to protect the anonymity of the social services departments, individuals cannot be named but we are very grateful for their help.

One of the experiments was undertaken with the help of Phyllida Parsloe, now Professor emeritus at the University of Bristol, and the larger enterprise depended on the efforts of several other Unit researchers and support staff, including Elizabeth Brown, Debbie Doyle, Heather Leitch, Yvonne McCann, Sue Moyers and Harriet Ward. Those wishing to know more about scientific development work will want to read Harriet Ward's own account of the implementation of the *Looking After Children* materials.

Before an account of any Dartington projects is published, we look to outsiders to review the work in draft. We were particularly fortunate in this case to have had the comments of Celia Atherton, Chris Davies, Jane Gibbons, Roy Parker, Spencer Millham and June Thoburn.

Finally, we owe a debt of gratitude to Carolyn Davies in the Research Development Division of the Department of Health and to her colleagues in policy divisions, particularly Norman Duncan, Elizabeth Johnson and Wendy Rose. This book is about a series of experimental ventures to learn about the application of research findings; it owes much to the support and encouragement of these four people.

# Introduction

Publications from social research units are usually about social issues, such as delinquency or adoption. This book is rather different: it is about an aspect of research activity which not long ago would have been considered rather peripheral, namely the development and translation of findings to make them useful to professionals and practitioners in social work and social policy.

Development work is frequently the close neighbour of research, but the two are seldom combined in the same exercise. More normally when a scientist discovers something or has a bright idea, it will be left to someone else to exploit its potential, leaving the scientist free to tackle another project. Perhaps as a result, British social scientists are actually considered rather poor at development work. Whether it is fair criticism to say so or simply the sign of an historical prejudice, for those who work in the area of applied research the conventional separation of roles, responsibilities and abilities has become a hindrance. One reason for writing this book has been to review the separation of roles and to suggest something more appropriate to the times.

By definition, the readership for a publication of this sort must be small, but as the relationship between research and practice changes so, we think, the need for appraisals of this kind will increase. The Dartington Unit's experience should be of interest, for example, to those who fund research with the object of ensuring that it is applied to policy and practice, also to those in government, for example the social services inspectorate or local and health authorities, who regard it as part of their task to disseminate research. Then there is a small but expanding group of specialist centres which will no doubt develop similar work into new areas, and workers in other fields of the personal social services and in health and education who are also trying to apply the messages of science. For quite a wide range of specialist readers there may be something here that strikes a chord.

The book's aims are straightforward: first to outline the various development projects undertaken at Dartington during the last 15 years, second, to give any evidence of success or failure, third, to summarise the results and suggest some future directions for those who wish to develop their research using similar methods.

Spin-offs from the Unit's experience are also reported. For example, the testing of materials and tools has produced some good indications of what social workers know and

The authors are keenly aware of the narrowness of the readership for a book of this kind: it includes chapters about approaches to publication design which may be of little interest to most researchers and detailed descriptions of an approach to research which researchers may find illuminating but which will leave most designers cold. Each chapter begins with a brief description of contents to help the unwary and page headings are offered as an aid to selective reading.

where they obtain their information. Consequently we are beginning to know better how professionals use research, a matter of keen concern to those in other professions, not least in medicine, where the pursuit of an evidence base by front-line workers such as general practitioners has become more determined in recent years. One might say, with the benefit of hindsight, that finding out how people obtain and use knowledge, or applying the lessons already learned in other fields should have been a first consideration for this activity, but sometimes researchers choose to remain as ignorant of research as the professionals they seek to influence.

In seeking to review the Unit's interest in development work, the scope of the survey is limited to projects whose chief aim has been to bring research evidence directly to bear on practice. (As will be seen, this is not the only type of connection that can be made between the two worlds.)

The projects discussed are :

- The *Going Home* materials for managers, social workers and parents, which seek to ensure that children looked after are returned home in appropriate circumstances and that reunions are as successful as possible.

- *Looking After Children*, a package of materials designed to help social workers collect information, make plans, review progress and monitor outcomes for children looked after away from home. The project materials also include a training pack, a computer programme, manuals, readers and handbooks. Its work among local authorities has been supported by a training programme, telephone advice lines and further research to help local authorities with planning. *Looking After Children* was not a Unit project as such but its involvement in designing the materials was a major concern in 1994 and 1995.

- Certain other developments, for example *Matching Needs and Services,* which seeks to help local authorities identify and plan for the needs of the children they support and *Child Protection: Messages from Research* which summarises the principal findings of a number of investigations and makes them accessible to a wide practice community.

The *Looking After Children* forms were designed and developed in association with colleagues from the universities of Bristol, Bath and Swansea, the National Children's Bureau and other agencies in the child care field.

# I The changing scene

This chapter describes some of the background to the Dartington's unit's interest in the links between research, social policy making and social work practice. It outlines its own attempts to tailor dissemination work to the needs of different readerships and the evolution of a view of development work as an influence on the way research is conceived and undertaken.

The Dartington Unit has always tried to make research findings relevant to the process of policy making and some modest claims can be made for its effectiveness over the years. For example, the 1978 study *Locking Up Children* was an influence on government policy which limited the number of local authority secure beds to around 300. *Lost in Care* paralleled a series of Department of Health attempts to change the way social workers regarded access between children absent in care and their relatives and which were consolidated by the *Children Act, 1989*. From time to time the Unit has dipped its own fingers in the waters of practice. The choice of Dartington as a location after early days at Cambridge reflected the team's early desire to apply ideas learned from education studies to the contemporary issue of integrating the independent and state education sectors. At the time, Dartington Hall School was one of the more enduring examples of pre-war educational experiment.

All that apart, it might be said that the Unit's specific interest in the link between research and social work practice stems from a seminar

David Donnison *Research for Policy*, Minerva 10, 1972

convened on behalf of the Department of Health in 1983, at a time when two potentially conflicting ideas about the purpose of social research were in circulation. One was derived from the Rothschild report of 1972 by which a research worker was regarded as a technologist who provided goods commissioned by a decision maker; the other, then considered more relevant, came from Donnison who had argued that research was meant to illuminate opinion, enable policy makers to orient themselves and create a climate for action. The renewed emphasis on 'getting through' pointed to some combination of both attitudes: the broad purpose of social research might be said to provide the wherewithal to illuminate opinion, enable policy makers to orient themselves and to underpin and inform good practice.

Whatever the rationale, conveying research messages to practitioners was ceasing to be simply a matter of accumulating material in case the need for communication should arise. New obligations were beginning to be added to research contracts. It was not enough that a research report should be communicable: there was to be a strategy for

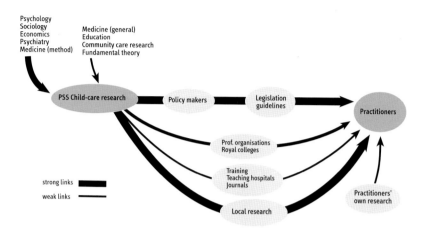

Psychology
Sociology
Economics
Psychiatry
Medicine (method)

Medicine (general)
Education
Community care research
Fundamental theory

PSS Child-care research

Policy makers

Legislation guidelines

Practitioners

Prof. organisations
Royal colleges

Training
Teaching hospitals
Journals

Practitioners' own research

Local research

strong links
weak links

When it gave evidence to the review of personal social services research published as the *Wider Strategy for Research and Development Relating to the Personal Social Services*, the Dartington Unit compared the various links between research and practice. As the diagram illustrates, the quickest and surest route is to get the findings to the policy makers, who, where appropriate, implement new legislation and/or guidelines. The long route via local research can also have its impact. Other avenues are less well charted, particularly in comparison with the professional corridors of influence that exist for example in the worlds of psychology, psychiatry and other branches of medicine.

In a lecture at the University of Bristol in 1992, the Dartington Unit's former director Spencer Millham spoke about the changing relationship he had witnessed between research and policy in the course of his career and the conclusion it had driven him towards: 'Social work does not seem to me to be a profession where research evidence and conclusions are accepted automatically. I find that research conclusions, along with many other things, are "negotiable", that is, subject to perspective, interest and discussion. Research is treated as if it were one perspective among many, which some people can have but others may disregard. This attitude on the part of social workers may be due to a lack of training or a training that emphasises empathy and intuition rather than authority of knowledge. On the other hand, it may be due to a misapprehension on the part of social workers that one of the key characteristics of a profession is autonomy and autonomous decision making. Or it may simply reflect a lack of accountability.'

disseminating the results and for that to happen a readership needed to be identified at the outset, preferably one not confined to the larger community of one's peers.

There is an important distinction to be made between *policy making* and *practice*. In 1983 the links between research and policy making in the Dartington Unit's field were already fairly strong, to the extent that when Sir William Utting, the chief inspector of social services, came to write the preface to the *Children Act*, 1989 he was able to say that the new legislation was informed by research evidence in almost every line. But as the relationship between research and policy has matured, research and *practice* and, for that matter, researcher and practitioner have often seemed to be at odds with one another.

The uncertainty of the routes and connections between the two realms persists, but the response has tended to be less one of criticism than a search for practical solutions. The 1994 Department of Health document, *A Wider Strategy for Research and Development Relating to the Personal Social Services* captured the prevailing mood, noting:

> It is often assumed that the social services lack a research culture. We have found that motivation is not the problem but access. Access to and use of research findings requires attention to be paid to the process as well as the outcome. (p.4)

This is a book largely about process based on the Unit's search for a useful relationship between research and practice. Essentially, research is considered to have three functions: first to develop an idea, encourage professionals to think in a new way or consider their practice in the light of new

1 The heart of the *Looking After Children* materials is a series of six age-related Assessment and Action Records, which provide a means of monitoring a child's development with respect to health, education, identity, family and social relationships, social presentation, emotional and behavioural development and self-care skills. There is also a series of planning and review forms, parts of which have been computerised by the Social Services Research and Development Unit at Bath University. The Unit's involvement first in the revision, later in the design and production of the materials is described on page 31.

Ward, H. (ed.) *Looking After Children: Research into Practice* (The Second Report to the Department of Health on Assessing Outcomes in Child Care), HMSO, London, 1995

2 The range of *Going Home* materials included the book, *Going Home: the return of children separated from their families*, research summaries, a booklet of checklists for professionals to complete on all separated children at different stages in their care careers, a guide for parents experiencing separation and return and an experimental computer programme for team leaders wishing to audit patterns of separation and return in their area. The Unit's involvement in the production of the materials is described in more detail on pages 40-45. Other experimental work, such as the involvement of an experienced professor of social work in one location and training days in others is described in chapters 8 and 9.

empirical findings; second, to help a professional make a decision and to be analytical when contemplating the likely consequences of different actions; third and more simply, to impart information. Since the 1983 seminar, Dartington has attempted development work in each of the areas just mentioned.

1 The most important project in the first category, that of developing an idea, is *Looking After Children* which, at its root, is about encouraging professionals to consider outcome as a concept and, more specifically, the quality of the interventions fashioned on behalf of children looked after. Little will be said about the project here as it is well reported elsewhere in Ward. Other examples of work in the area being tested are *Matching Needs and Services* which is intended to help planners understand the idea of 'need' and *Structure and Cultures in Residential Children's Homes*, which is designed to help managers of residential care understand the connections between the concepts of structure, culture and outcome (in relation to a children's home and to the individual child).

2 The second area of activity is best characterised by the *Going Home* materials which are extensively reviewed later. Published in 1993, *Going Home* charted the experiences of 875 children looked after and established factors which, in combination, best predict whether a child is likely to return to live with relatives and, if so, indicate the likely success of the reunion. The research design spawned several developmental tools aimed at improving professional decision making.

The *Going Home* research study explored the return home of children looked after by local authorities. Its aims were:

- to clarify the nature of return by exploring all the relevant literature
- to examine the different routes by which children in care are returned to their families
- to investigate children's experiences of the process, concentrating on the differences between households and varying styles and levels of social work support
- to identify groups of children particularly vulnerable to re-abuse, placement breakdown, behaviour problems and family rejection
- to highlight factors that can make a significant contribution to successful return and give social workers practical advice on how best to prepare and manage children's return

The research combined quantitative and qualitative approaches. The quantitative work drew on and extended the follow-up of cohorts of children assembled for studies such as *Lost In Care*, *Trials and Tribulations* and *Secure Treatment Outcomes*. It showed which children returned home, when and why. It also provided information on the success of reunions.

The qualitative work followed the progress of 31 children from 24 families selected to cover the range of return patterns. This scrutiny, which continued for 18 months from the point at which return became an issue, provided evidence on the process of return and the reasons for success and failure. Seven episodes were analysed to illustrate the process: separation, change in family and child

circumstances, the time when return becomes an issue, the first days at home, the honeymoon, the row and a new *modus vivendi*.

Findings from the two sets of studies were then incorporated into checklists of factors which in combination best predicted a child's likelihood of return home at different points in his or her care career and the success of any reunion.

For the first edition of the checklists, published in 1992, five questionnaires were compiled. They were to be completed at the time of the child's separation, in the month following separation, for children away from home after six months and when a child had been away from home for two years. The fifth checklist dealt with the prospects for reunion.

An important aim of the subsequent developmental phase of the study was to test the validity of the checklists by applying them to looked after children at the point of separation and to compare predictions indicated by their circumstances to what actually occurred, in other words, to the outcomes for children and their families. Eight local authorities took part in this exercise and 462 children were studied. One of the eight was unable to sustain its involvement; a ninth participated in the part of the exercise designed to assess the effects on practice of using the instruments, but was not involved in the validation of the predictive factors. Thus a fairly robust instrument was produced. It was based on a blind application to looked after children and followed up prospectively.

*Trial and Tribulations: Returning children from local authority care to their families (Farmer, E. and Parker R. HMSO, London, 1991) was a Bristol University study.*

*A summation of the secure treatment work, Secure Treatment Outcomes: The Care Careers of Very Difficult Adolescents (Bullock, R., Little, M. and Millham, S.) was published in the Dartington Social Research Series by Ashgate in 1998*

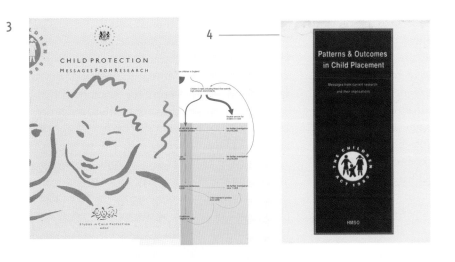

3

4

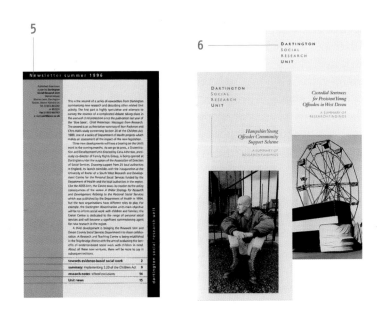

5

6

**3, 4** The third category of Unit development work, the imparting of research information is exemplified by *Child Protection: Messages from Research* which assembled the principal messages from 20 studies, mainly funded by the Department of Health and was the result of long consultation with the authors of the studies it covered and testing against the specialist knowledge of a multi-disciplinary advisory group. It was the third in a series of review publications produced by the Department of Health since the 1983 seminar, the others being *Social Work Decisions in Child Care* (1986) and *Patterns and Outcome in Child Placement* (1991), referred to elsewhere as the 'pink books'.

Other publications under the same heading are of a kind familiar to any organisation that tries to keep its customers, clients or consumers informed about its work. There is a newsletter associated with the *Looking After Children* project and one for the Unit's work as a whole. **5** Synopses have been produced of the Unit's books **6** and in some cases summaries of findings have been styled for particular constituencies–for instance for subscribers to *The Magistrate* magazine and members of the Judicial Studies Board.

Everything in the three categories has been an extension of some aspect of the Unit's research, distinguishing it from much other development work that casts more widely for its knowledge base. Furthermore, there has been an increasingly explicit intention to link the theory underpinning the research with that driving the development work. Ideas of career, process and episode that are

The theory in *Child Protection: Messages from Research,* turned on the relationship between definitions of abuse, the process of intervention and the outcomes of services. The declared intention had been that it should distil empirical results into a form useful to practitioners, but it attracted the criticism that policy was being influenced by the theory the publication contained.

Another rather less obvious aspect of the practical relationship between research and development work will also be explored here–the extent to which publications of different kinds can extend, strengthen and so help to validate the research from which they are derived. It is worth stating at the outset that this book is not about making a smart job of publishing research, nor even entirely about how research is best applied to practice. Rather it tries to describe a relationship between research and development in which each gives energy and originality to the other. *Child Protection: Messages from Research* generated as many messages *for* research as it released into the world of practice.

integral to the design of the *Going Home* checklists, for example, are carried through in the guide produced for parents. Conversely, when *Child Protection: Messages from Research* came to be written, some middle range theory needed to be developed to rationalise the mass of data and the summaries of other people's research.

However malleable the links between research and development, none of the innovations to be described in this book would have been possible without the technology that has become generally available during the same 15 years and the readiness of funders to invest in the expertise necessary to make use of it. Technology is a two-edged sword, of course. It has multiplied the publishing routes open to social research, but at the same time generated heaps of data high and wide enough to obscure any fragile truth from view. It has also made it possible for research to exploit a range of media, for example including video conferencing, but it is increasingly difficult under these new conditions to protect the authority of scientific evidence or to offer an effective appraisal of everything in circulation.

Complications aside, the key questions for research development continue to be about the effectiveness of dissemination strategies. From that perspective, *Going Home* may be an important example because it attempted to make the development work integral to the original research design. Previously, development had been an optimistic afterthought on the part of those who managed to maintain some enthusiasm for a project to which they had already devoted three years of their life, but the checklists, parents' guide

and computer programme associated with *Going Home* were conceived, in principle at least, at the point at which the research was commissioned and the results collected during the development phase were intended to improve the scientific design.

The first part of the investigation, published in 1993, was based on retrospectively collected data on 875 children entering care. The second part is grounded in results collected from the prospectively applied–and therefore more reliable–developmental checklists used with 463 children being looked after. As it turned out, the design had other research benefits because the first set of data was assembled prior to the implementation of the *Children Act,* 1989, whereas the second describes the situation since.

Just as illuminating has been the opportunity to consider the impact of the *Going Home* developments on professionals, children and families, so that several questions previously unanswered by research are dealt with. They include: Are developmental tools used and, if so, are they applied appropriately? Do developments like *Going Home* lead to better social work decisions? And, crucially, is there any evidence that the exercises improve outcomes for children and families?

It will be shown that development work has begun to change the way research is conceived and that, carefully designed, studies fashioned with their extension in mind need be no less scientific and can contribute to the rigorous testing of research. Evaluation of the impact of research developments on professional practice and children's lives is changing, too; if nothing else it has become more focused. Gone is the grape-shot approach, when a range of materials was fired vaguely skywards in the hope that one or two pellets would make a hit, but there is still some way to go before information is precisely matched to its target audience. In this respect, research dissemination still lacks some of the expertise of commercial advertising.

Technical refinements of the sort described here will continue to have limited effect while the circumstances of research and practice remain so separate. Those in social work research seldom have practice qualifications and usually no intention of ever practising. One of the benefits of making use of tools such as *Going Home, Looking After Children* and *Matching Needs and Services* is that they give professionals an insight into the theory and method of research. In a more advanced form, they should make good research simpler and more accessible. Similarly, because applying the tools necessarily draws researchers into the realities of the practitioners' world and into a relationship with social workers, they learn how taxing supporting vulnerable children and their families can be–that the task is seldom amenable to the laboratory conditions of science and that there may be plausible reasons why people do not behave as researchers expect.

Merton, R.K. *Social Theory and Social Structure,* Glencoe, Free Press, 1957

The adjective 'scientific' is central to the development work described in this book. The scientific method requires researchers to relate factors by hypothesising that if a, then b under conditions c, and to test the strength of the prediction by repeated applications under the same and different sets of conditions.

In social sciences, causal investigations are complicated by the different meaning that apparently similar situations have for those involved and the difficulty of replicating social situations. Merton argues that this makes individual research designs inevitably subjective. However, objectivity is achieved by the institutional structure of science, namely the pursuit of knowledge directed by values of universalism, organised scepticism, communal ownership and economic disinterestedness.

The Dartington Unit would also argue that the research methods used to analyse qualitative evidence are just as rigorous as those brought to quantitative data. Both sets of methods have a role depending on the theory that drives the research.

# 2 The place of evidence in social work

In this chapter, some contradictions in the relationship between research and practice are explored in more detail. There is a discussion of the influences on social work practice and how they have developed over recent years. Since evidence is only one aspect of that changing equation, more innovative ways of linking research and practice are considered, in order to identify the role of 'scientific development work' more clearly.

The *Children Act,* 1989 and the accompanying guidance are a clear illustration of the extent to which theory and contemporary empirical findings concerning child care research have been incorporated into policy. Similar influences are as visible in policy concerning adoption and child protection (rather less so in juvenile offending) and in the official reports of the Social Services Inspectorate, the Department of Health and the Audit Commission. The enthusiasm among policy makers for research ideas may be constrained by financial and political considerations but the attention paid to the evidence, in England and Wales at least, is beyond dispute.

The relationships between research and practice, also between policy and practice are more obscure. As Roy Parker noted in 1989, 'In discussions about the contribution that research can make, policy and practice are often treated as if they were one and the same. This is misleading because it is plain that the connection between research and policy and that between research and practice are markedly different. Indeed, if we are to understand the difficulties that surround the application of research results to practical affairs the nature of this

difference is of the utmost importance.'

The very nature of social work as a profession bears on the relationship between research and practice. In 1975 Etzioni described it as a 'semi-profession', whose members tended to work inside bureaucracies. Unlike medicine or law, there is little tradition in social work of referring difficult cases upwards: there are no specialist centres and little notion of senior practice. Senior social work staff are more likely to be managers than senior practitioners and only a handful of professionals undertake research. Some would say that the social services bureaucracy has a tendency to stifle one of social work's best characteristics, namely the value it accords to individual judgement based on experience and knowledge. In point of fact, the bureaucracy may just as often shield its senior staff from pressures to provide answers to practice questions.

The absence of a common conceptual framework also hampers the ability of social work practice to absorb research. Among lawyers there may be disagreements concerning the interpretation of the law, but, generally speaking, there is agreement on the legal principles that are

Roy Parker, whose name occurs several times in this section, is Professor emeritus of social policy at the University of Bristol and a fellow of the Centre for Social Policy: Warren House. He was a member of the Seebohm Committee and, in the 1970s, of the DHSS Children's Research Liaison Group. His numerous publications include *Away from Home: A History of Child Care,* Barnardos, 1990, *Change, Choice and Conflict in Social Policy,* Heinemann, 1975 and *In Whose Trust? A report of the Jasmine Beckford Inquiry,* National Foster Care Association, 1988.

As long ago as 1966 Roy Parker produced a tool which indicated to social workers which children were at greatest risk of foster home breakdown. Twenty years later, armed with more sophisticated methods made possible by advances in computer science, Berridge and Cleaver (*Foster Home Breakdown*, Blackwell, *1987)* did much the same. Many professionals know about this work, but few are likely to consult it prior to making a placement decision. Similarly, few youth justice workers will turn to West and Farrington's studies prior to composing a pre-sentence report. Told that nearly half of children with special needs placed for adoption in their tenth year later separated from their new parents, a senior judge asked ' how am I to know whether the case before me is in the half that will succeed or the half that will fail?' Should he have been expected to know that June Thoburn's research, on which these findings are based, provides a reasonably reliable answer?

Gibbons, J. and Tunstill. J. 'A Review of good dissemination initiatives' unpublished report to the Department of Health, 1993

MacDonald, G. and Roberts, H. *What Works in the Early Years: Effective interventions for children and their families in health, social welfare, education and child protection*, Barnardos, 1995

applied. In medicine, a general practitioner's knowledge differs from that of a surgeon, but they share a very similar understanding of human physiology. These underpinnings have no direct equivalent in social work. In fact, training courses frequently make a virtue of the dissimilarities, for instance between community social work and case-work. Little wonder hard-pressed practitioners struggle to find the right questions to ask of research and cannot always interpret the answers they are offered.

Researchers deserve a share of reproach, too. Social workers often remark how little of what they read is directly applicable to practice. **Gibbons and Tunstill** found that research was often presented in an unusable form and thrust upon social workers as if they were to be treated as passive consumers whose task was simply to apply findings. And, while it is true to say that there is more research in circulation than practitioners can reasonably be expected to read, there are still fundamental gaps in what is on offer. Scarcely any evidence has been assembled on the result in particular circumstances of taking no action, and findings on the effects of different interventions on similar conditions collected by means of random allocation studies are scarce, as **MacDonald and Roberts's** recent study clearly demonstrates. One of the purposes of this review is to assess what is useful to practitioners delivered by which media and in what style.

At a theoretical level the links between research and practice are of course fairly direct. It would be surprising, for example, if a qualified practising social worker was found to be unaware of the

significance in children's lives of cognitive development or the importance of their attachment to birth parents. Even if incompletely understood, such concepts are part of the professional language. Similarly, the diminishing role of psychoanalytic theory in social work training may have altered the climate of practice but such ideas are still a vital part of practitioners' thinking. Bowlby's melodies linger long after the hammer blows of competence tests have died away.

The link between *empirical* research and practice is another matter. Findings based on the experiences of many thousands of children of course attract attention. The discovery that nearly nine out of ten separated children return home and that some will do so contrary to the wishes of social workers, will surely have some effect on practice, assuming that it is made widely known. If professionals know that the most likely outcome for a looked after child, whatever his or her circumstance, is reunion with relatives, their professional behaviour will change—as later chapters demonstrate. By the same means, recognition of the risks of placement breakdown in residential care, foster homes and adoptive placements and concepts of drift and planning blight have entered the professional psyche. But there is relatively little to suggest a direct connection between research evidence and the work of the individual practitioner; even distinguished practitioners are on the whole reluctant to explain their practice or to subject it to testing by research.

Naturally enough, most efforts to improve the relationship between research and practice have

Take as an example, findings on drift produced by Lydia Lambert and Jane Rowe in their 1973 study of children under the age of ten in local authority care. The idea coincided with a body of knowledge from the United States that suggested that 'permanency' either in the family home or in a substitute setting was a vital ingredient of good outcomes for children looked after away from home. Rowe and Lambert's findings were soon applied to adolescents; permanency was interpreted to mean just placement away from home. The synthesis of ideas and misapplied evidence resulted in many older children being adopted, which, as we now know, is a high risk strategy.

A manifestation of the misunderstanding that can occur when data from different sources are married together came in reactions to a research overview Dartington prepared for judges. The six page guide was designed to meet a request from the Judicial Studies Board that it should fit in a judge's inside pocket. It condensed a range of evidence including that on patterns of return and adoption breakdown. It was first distributed in draft form at a conference for judges at which a QC and family court judge independently came to the conclusion that it must be better to adopt children when they are young and soon after they are separated from home—practically the opposite of the view taken by those more familiar with the research studies.

been aimed at general practice. Significant strides have been made by the Department of Health in the last decade with the dissemination of the research overviews mentioned in the previous section. The Association of Directors of Social Services has set up Research in Practice, an initiative to develop research findings for the benefit of subscribing local authorities, and there is also a regional research and development programme in the South West, the Centre for Evidence-based Social Services, which is being jointly funded by the Department of Health and local authorities. The Family Support Network at the Universities of East Anglia and Keele and the continuing work of organisations such as the National Children's Bureau are other examples of initiatives that are taking a broad approach.

A possible exception to the tendency to deal in generalities rather than seek to influence the behaviour of individual social workers is represented by the extent of the Department of Health's support for the *Looking After Children* materials, which by the end of 1998 will have been implemented in 90% of English local authorities, translated into Welsh by the Welsh Office and used abroad. The *Looking After Children* approach links different aspects of children's lives: their identity, education, social functioning and so forth and is designed to ensure that someone takes proper responsibility for their monitoring and development. On the face of it, *Looking After Children* is very widely applicable, not only among local authorities but also inside voluntary agencies and organisations who may struggle, for example to take into account evidence of homelessness,

recidivism and child protection when deciding what to do on behalf of a runaway who has several convictions and is also making disclosures about having been sexually abused. But the materials were criticised on the grounds that they mechanised social work and undervalued careful judgement.

These examples shed some light on the contrasting aspirations of social workers and researchers. As Parker noted, the former seek to apply general findings to particular cases, whereas the latter seek to generalise from individual situations. No wonder it is difficult to produce material that satisfies both camps and that research results are so often misinterpreted.

Communication between researchers and social workers is hindered further by contrasting working practices. Researchers are inclined to hedge their findings—to the annoyance of practitioners who very often have to commit themselves to decisions that can have profound consequences for vulnerable children. On the other hand, there is a tendency for social workers to regard as extraordinary cases that researchers consider routine, and vice versa: for example, funders will pay for research into child murderers or victims of Munchausen's Syndrome by Proxy when a typical practitioner will probably come across a single instance of either only once or twice in an entire career.

It is not the intention to argue that research knowledge can ever be the sole influence on social work practice or that some pure form of knowledge exists that is not itself influenced by general social pressures. There is, for example, a moral aspect to any deliberations concerning children's lives which, to a point, is subsumed in legislation, regulations and the accumulating force of important court rulings. Changing morality has borne on modern attitudes to vulnerable children since the introduction of the Poor Law and the national conscience will sometimes be moved by moral persuaders such as Barnardo and Stephenson.

There is also what might be called a pragmatic dimension to be reckoned with, derived from the politics of the possible. Following the death of Denis O'Neill at the hands of his foster parents and the enormous public outcry that followed, the report of Myra Curtis, the *Children Act, 1948* ushered in an era influenced as much by judgments about what it was possible to do as what ought to be done.

A third influence on practice is the consumer perspective which began to be a factor in the late 70s and the early 80s. Particularly influential was the publication of *Who Cares?*, an anthology of comments from children in care. The establishment of the Family Rights Group in 1975 was another of its manifestations and the creation of *ChildLine* a decade later may prove to have been the apotheosis of a trend. The voice of the consumer speaks directly to practice, for example in the desire of children to buy their own clothes or in a parent's need to see absent offspring and also raises fundamental questions about children's and parents' rights. Such developments have coincided with the UN Convention of the Rights of the Child and the increasing interest of the European Court of Human Rights in domestic policy.

These three influences on practice are not necessarily complementary nor do they necessarily work in the same direction at any given moment, and while this is not the place for lengthy speculation, it is worth considering the complexity of the process of interaction between stronger or weaker moral and pragmatic forces in society, or between consumers fighting a new cause and researchers feebly urging caution. If social workers were to be guided by moral concerns alone, would their interventions be more or less practical? As a nation, we might introduce a law against smacking children, on the basis that there is a substantial body of opinion that believes smacking is wrong, but since nine out of ten parents hit their children, how would it be possible to enforce the legislation? And what might be the unintended consequence of prosecuting a mother who lost her temper because her three-year-old threw a carton of orange juice across an aisle at Sainsburys?

Or what if practical considerations alone were to rule social workers' lives? Barnardo was a practical man, who saw a need and did something about it. But the response was not uniform across the country and children's moral rights were undoubtedly neglected. Barnardo believed he acted in the best interests of children, but his interventions had damaging effects on the lives of some of those he believed he 'saved', not least on those who were forcibly emigrated to Canada or Australia.

If, on the other hand, practice was entirely driven by evidence, what would happen to people like Barnardo? And would not the moral conscience of the nation shudder when help was refused to a fourth-time offender because there was no technology available that was known to relieve his or her condition? Similarly, in a world so dominated by research, it is conceivable that a young victim of sexual abuse would be refused treatment on the grounds that there was too little evidence that current interventions made any difference to long-term outcomes. What should be the response to an adolescent's expressed wish for residential care when independent research suggests that his or her needs are likely to be aggravated by such a placement?

In Dartington's experience, legislation, practical concerns and the consumer perspective become enmeshed in research, but not always in a rational or easily predictable way. In some studies, evidence is represented by a consumer voice, as in *The*

*Hothouse Society*, in Siobhan Kelly's contribution to *A Life without Problems?* or parents' quotations in *Lost in Care* or *Access Disputes in Child Care*. To complicate matters further, in some cases practice has been directly affected by the science embedded in development projects as in the case of the *Going Home* materials reviewed here, and very occasionally researchers will contribute directly to policy and practice formulation, for example by helping to write the 1983 code of practice, *Access to Children in Care* or preparing *Child Protection: Messages from Research*.

The publication in 1966 of Parker's *Decision in Child Care* may be said to mark the moment when the usefulness of research evidence began to be understood, soon followed by the Seebohm Report which represented a breakthrough because

Seminal works are sometimes as much the product of a particular climate as an influence on climate change. So while it seems right to speak of the importance of *Decision in Child Care*, as a work in tune with changing times, alas it was not widely used, for all the reasons described in this book.

There are at least four influences on social work practice: there is the moral/legal aspect, bound up in legislation; there is the pragmatic aspect, marking out what is possible; there is the consumer view; and then there is evidence – which represents just one aspect of the equation. The balance between these influences will change with time. The diagram on the right is not designed to be definitive, but it is a reasonably accurate representation of the relationship between the four dimensions during the 20th century.

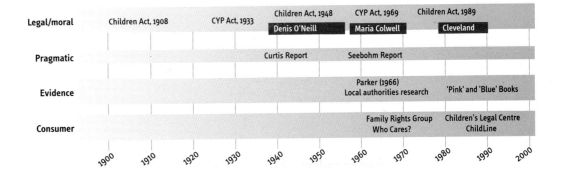

## ▶ the usefulness of thresholds

Another way of illustrating the way moral, legal and pragmatic influences bear on practice is to consider how social workers decide whether to act, when to act, how to act and when to withdraw in cases of child protection. The evidence which underpins the 'Blue Book' found that a single incident is rarely sufficient to trigger professional concern as contextual factors are so important. The debate over the rights and wrongs of smacking exemplifies this. Practitioners also have to take into account any independent evidence that indicates what is bad for children. Research has highlighted the dangers of shaking a baby and the deleterious effects of low warmth, high criticism environments on children's development. Practice wisdom has also accumulated from the revelations of abuse inquiries. In deciding whether to take any action, social workers have to consider all these issues.

To help them do this, professionals draw a threshold; this involves deciding the point beyond which a behaviour or parenting style can be considered harmful and the point beyond which it becomes necessary for the state to take action. Thresholds are placed at different stages of the protection process, such as when to enquire, when to visit, when to conference, when to separate children from their families or limit access between them. An examination of child care policy and practice over the last century would suggest that thresholds change. For child abuse, they have generally been lowered to uncover a greater amount of abuse and to intervene in more cases. For young offenders, thresholds have mostly moved in the opposite direction with less professional response and policies of diverting youngsters away from criminal justice systems.

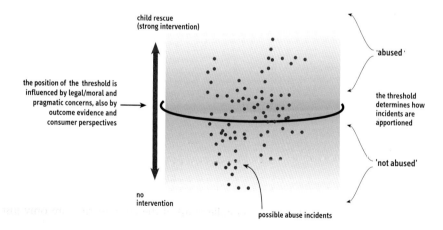

child rescue
(strong intervention)

the position of the threshold is influenced by legal/moral and pragmatic concerns, also by outcome evidence and consumer perspectives

'abused'

the threshold determines how incidents are apportioned

'not abused'

no intervention

possible abuse incidents

## ▶ a glut of research literature

it indicated that research was to be regarded as a crucial contributor to the work of the new social services departments set up in 1971. At the outset, nearly every department employed research staff so that across the country around 300 were taken on. For a time there was a national association and a clearing house for publications, but most of the early provision was lost as priorities changed in the early 1980s. Then came the contract-dominated years of the mid-1980s when it is possible that initial uncertainty about value for money contributed to practitioners' wariness of research. The mood has since changed; it now pleases social services directors to say that they are succeeding in linking research and practice but it is not a new departure. The more telling point is that previously they were not the ones demanding the connection.

Forty years ago there was a mere handful of research studies of what we today call children in need. By reading them one could become expert in the literature overnight. Today there are literally hundreds of articles and books laden with research findings. It might once have been sufficient to allow this evidence to accumulate and periodically to summarise it for practitioners, as in case of the Pink and Blue Books; given time, a consensus about the implications empirical results have for practice will normally evolve. But lately researchers and managers have taken the discussion a stage further. They have begun to consider how the concepts which underpin empirical studies might be useful to social work practice and out of this deeper reappraisal process the term 'evidence-based' social work has emerged.

As this book goes to press, there is little

consensus about the definition of evidence-based social work. At Dartington it is taken to mean social work undertaken by a range of people (not just professional social workers) which is grounded in good knowledge of the needs of children and families and what the best research has to say about what works for which groups of children and why. Increasingly, such analysis extends to the cost-benefit of different interventions. Evidence based social work should provide a common conceptual framework into which new ideas, new evidence and new projects can be fitted and implies a balance between the legal/moral, pragmatic, evidential and consumer influences on practice just described.

Most of the evidence described in this book is in the form of facts and figures: it is empirical research. But, depending on one's point-of-view, evidence can take many other forms, broadly following the pattern of influences on social work already touched on. So, in the legal context there is case law in which the court's decision in one situation is used as a benchmark for similar future situations and moral influences may be represented for example in philosophical commentary or media analysis. Nor do the pragmatic actions of social work take place in a vacuum: accumulated experience represents a type of evidence potentially every bit as valid as the data of empirical research. The consumer view is also evidence-based and the directness of its appeal often brings potency to its voice.

What then is the proper place of evidence in development and dissemination activity? Until very recently the primary object has been to get empirical evidence to practitioners. In future, consideration will have to be given to the balance between the several kinds of evidence available.

Evidence-based social work makes other demands. It requires researchers to ask how studies are undertaken, how valid they are and who should undertake them. It also gives policy makers pause for thought: the discussion about the refocusing of children's services that accompanied the dissemination of Department of Health funded child protection research required a review of the *Children Act,* 1989 and the principles that underpin it. Training, too, has come under scrutiny. What evidence is taught on social work courses and how are qualified workers to know the value of one piece of research in the context of any particular aspect of practice?

The preoccupation with evidence is partly the product of increased dissemination and development work but the relationship between the two may nevertheless be problematic. As subsequent chapters will demonstrate, development tools have the potential to be research instruments–the *Going Home* checklists, *Looking After Children* materials and True for Us Exercises in *Child Protection: Messages from Research* are examples of what has already been achieved in this direction; but the strengths (for example, providing local authority planners with reliable data) and weaknesses (say, the risk of inconsistent data collection) of the combination are only just becoming apparent.

Attempts to provide social work with an evidence base from research have led directly to management tools like *Matching Needs and Services,*

*Structure and Culture in Residential Care* and *Looking After Children*, which can be used to plan children's services. Again, it needs to be said that the links between the concepts that underpin the instruments, of needs, thresholds, services and outcome are only now beginning to emerge, and they in turn will inform the emerging definition of evidence-based social work.

All this is bound to leave a series of loose ends, only a few of which can be dealt with here. Much will depend on the achievement during the next few years of the new, specialised centres, for example the Centre for Evidence-based Social Services at Exeter University, Research in Practice at Dartington and the NHS Centre for Reviews and Dissemination at York.

It is clear that research has a lower standing among those working directly with children and families than those who make policy, which directly affects practice. It is clear, too, that there are many obstacles between evidence and practice— uncertainties concerning the differing aspirations of researchers and social workers, the professional status of social work and the marginal interests of the research community. It is also apparent that evidence is, and must be, only one among several influences on practice.

All of which leads to new uncertainties. The question 'what evidence is an appropriate basis for social work' has only lately begun to be asked. The conceptual (as opposed to empirical) challenges research directs towards policy, training, practice, and, indeed, to the nature of evidence itself are only beginning to be recognised.

The promise of evidence-based social work may be short-lived. It would not be the first time that a challenge to social work had evaporated into the thin air from which it momentarily emerged. But the promise of a new emphasis in social work has led to widespread reflection on the nature of evidence, different types of social work research, the training of professionals and the formulation of policy.

# 3 Linking research and development work

This chapter returns to the Dartington Unit's portfolio as a basis for describing how ideas about dissemination have come to rest on the development and wide use of information technology and the growth of information design.

The evolution of the ideas that underpin evidence-based social work is being determined to a large extent by the momentum of scientific development work that has been added to the portfolios of research centres during the last decade. The change is not an altogether altruistic or passive response: there is more pressure on the research community to justify its claim to be contributing to knowledge about social problems. Funding bodies, too, are aware of the demand for practical effectiveness: they require research to be used and therefore to be widely disseminated. At every level, by some definition, the work must represent value for money.

Nor can the increasing interest in evidence on the part of social services departments be regarded as an uncomplicated strategy for improving services to children and families. Most industrialised countries are seeking to limit their public expenditure to 40% of GDP and the prudent use of evidence is regarded as a way of refining services in order to meet increasing demand on a fixed budget. Simple professional pride must also be a factor, for example when social workers seek to match the expertise of a guardian *ad litem* in court, Similarly, the aspiration to develop social work as a profession must play a part: since the Cleveland Inquiry a decade ago, when it was arguably in decline, social work has been at the fulcrum of child protection.

Broadly speaking, social policy research falls into three categories. First, there are theoretical studies which fashion concepts and incorporate them into larger perspectives; they are usually part of an academic discipline or sub-discipline. Second, there is large-scale empirical work which provides new information based upon reliable data. Such studies, which review situations and provide evidence to test hypotheses, have traditionally been the bread and butter of Units like Dartington. Third, there are evaluations of particular situations, client needs or professional practice. These are usually brief and limited in scope but they can be useful if they belong in a context of wider knowledge.

Each type of research has been undertaken at Dartington at different times, always on the premise that the distinctions between them are largely artificial. For example, large-scale empirical studies need to be guided by well-considered theories and theoretical work needs to draw on knowledge produced by empirical studies if its conclusions are to be accepted. Similarly, although quick evaluations are of limited value on their own, they are an important component of knowledge about services accumulated from theoretical and empirical work.

As the opening chapters have indicated, development work, too, can have several dimensions. It can involve drawing out policy and practice implications from research results and making recommendations about guidance and procedures, leading perhaps to the publication of a code of practice. Or it can generate indicators or checklists to help those making decisions, which may merely serve as *aides memoire* or may have predictive value, enabling decision makers to be more aware of the consequences of their actions. The dissemination of research findings in new and attractive ways can also be a legitimate developmental enterprise in its own right. Different types of research will always be of varying relevance to different types of development work, and *vice versa*.

In 1983, the year of the seminar on the Dissemination of Research Findings in Social Work, the Unit began a study of *Children's Homes.* Despite the fact that the seminar had demonstrated the weaknesses of existing arrangements, when the work was finished, it still seemed sufficient to publish a book, along with articles in professional and academic journals, that elaborated specific points. Conferences and training courses provided further opportunities to publicise the findings and–a radical step at the time–copies of the book were given away at a launch organised by the Social Care Association. The traditional methods were modified only slightly: findings were produced, reviewed and left to seep into accumulated wisdom. Next came *Foster Home Breakdown* and a similar strategy: since nearly all social workers and foster parents were likely to experience the kind of precipitate departure of a looked after child, it was considered reasonable to assume that professional concern and natural curiosity would be sufficient to attract a readership to the new knowledge the study was intended to provide.

Yet the 1983 seminar provided an abundance of evidence about the inefficiency of such an approach: it relied too much on the unrealistic expectation that social workers read journals and research reports. It was undermined by the pressures on contract researchers to draw a line under completed work, with little thought to its dissemination, and to move on the next paying project. The lack of any intermediary bodies such as the Royal Colleges in medicine to co-ordinate and publicise significant findings was another hindrance.

Signs of a response to the changing climate began to appear in 1985. Anxious to improve the dissemination of findings among practitioners, the DHSS, a major research funder in the child-care field, produced the first of the research overviews usually referred to as the 'Pink' and 'Blue' Books. *Social Work Decisions in Child Care,* the first 'pink book' which summarised the results of nine studies, was distributed to every child welfare agency in the country and was followed up by a series of national seminars for social workers at all levels of seniority.

A research note for designers

Research studies usually begin with an inkling of where gaps lie in existing knowledge. The focus might be on an explanation, for example 'why do children become delinquent?' or on an evaluation, such as 'what is the effectiveness of custodial sentences in stopping delinquency?' Sometimes the approach might be more akin to a monitoring exercise or an assessment of a service. The next step is to translate the questions into manageable issues so that when the explanations are eventually presented they will be relevant and comprehensible to the audiences they are designed for. An important part of the process is the application of what are called middle-range theories, sets of perspectives and interrelated concepts about social situations that have been found to be useful in previous work.

Middle-range theories have a workmanlike, spontaneous quality. Not only do they help to clarify the problem and develop hypotheses, they influence the explanations put forward.

The change in emphasis coincided with the completion of the next Dartington study, *Lost in Care*, an exploration of the problems of maintaining links between looked after children and their families. In the new climate, the Unit's original plan was to prepare guidance on managing access between separated children and their families, but it was pre-empted when the Department of Health invited the researchers to help prepare a code of practice of its own called *Access to Children in Care*. The code met the need for a practice guide based on academic studies (and so belonged to the first of the three categories of development work just mentioned). To take the development work a stage further, the Dartington Unit convened practitioner groups to consider the code in detail and recommend ways in which its proposals could be implemented. The results were published in *Access to Children in Care: Practitioners' Views*.

In retrospect, it may seem obvious that a Code of Practice has the potential to disseminate the main findings of a research study more efficiently than an unexpurgated research report, but at the time it was a fairly novel approach. The exercise brought fresh insights to the problem of organising contact and access, aspects of which were later incorporated into the more extensive guidance that accompanied the *Children Act* 1989. It also drew attention to ambiguities, introduced practice hints and brought a degree of sophistication to a publication designed to link theory, research and practice. But there was a limit to what could be achieved: since there was no indication at the outset of how well the Code of Practice would be used and nothing in law to compel practitioners to adopt its recommendations, team leaders were inclined to ignore it; the practitioner groups, meanwhile managed to add little to the ideas expressed in *Lost In Care* or the Code.

The early forays were less than satisfactory for other reasons, too. There was a disconcerting lack of theoretical underpinning to what was being attempted and no way of gauging the effect, unless one was to rely on anecdote. Indeed, in those days, there were few criteria by which success or failure could be evaluated. Because of the *ad hoc* way dissemination work tended to be organised, it did not always reach a wide audience, it could not easily be replicated and some groups, such as those training social work professionals, managed to avoid the initiatives altogether.

In the case of *Lost in Care*, as with its predecessors, there was no equivalent in the dissemination strategy to the middle-range theory that drove the empirical research. Development work was contemplated in detail only after the study was complete, by which time the overriding concern was simply to ensure that the findings were published.

Thereafter, first in relation to *Going Home* and *Looking After Children*, attempts began to be made to make the planning of the development work an integral part of the research design. In both studies, establishing the connection in the early stages eventually made it possible to produce development tools—checklists, questionnaires, forms and guides—that contributed to social work practice and permitted good practice to be assessed.

A second feature was the way conceptual links between research and development were maintained. For example, in the *Going Home* study, the research findings highlighted the importance of continuities in family life and their significance as a factor in decision-making with respect to separation and return and in the success or otherwise of child care plans. The theoretical design of the *Looking After Children* Assessment and Action Records also incorporated ideas about continuity and urged practitioners and family members to reconsider the implications of separation and return. The effectiveness of the exercises was then tested against common criteria. The *Going Home* developments included two experiments to discover which aspects of the tools made an impact on social workers' behaviour and which on outcomes for children and families (see chapter nine). In *Looking After Children* elaborate comparisons were made between samples of children inside and outside the looked after population–work described in the second report, *Looking After Children: Research into Practice*.

Greater precision coincided with widening scope. Previously, in order to maintain standards, development work was restricted to a narrow geographical area. For example, the practical work described in *Access to Children in Care* involved setting up a Family Support Group near Dartington and producing leaflets for the parents of children in a particular residential home. The initiative was reasonably successful in context but proved difficult to extend or replicate. In more recent projects, the catchment area has been wider but the target group has remained well defined:

*Going Home* included separate materials for social workers and parents while *Looking After Children* sought the participation of professionals, carers, parents and children throughout the process.

Heightened interest in scientific development work has led to a general recognition that those for whom the materials are intended obtain their information from a number of sources and that in order to influence practice, several different types of instrument need to be produced. In the *Going Home* work, many parents were influenced by the decision-making tool prepared for social workers and some practitioners found it helpful to complete the schedules with parents and children. Conversely, social workers were sometimes influenced by the advice booklet designed for parents. In each case a string of design decisions had been made about how best to present information to the different readerships; some of the calculations were informed by work with user groups, but most were intuitive. At the time nothing much was known about what social work professionals read or why or about the value or proper means of matching materials to the needs of different readerships. Both minefields are crossed in later chapters.

As for the value of design and the role of the designer in relation to scientific development work, it needs to be borne in mind that before 1983 it would have been impractical for a small research organisation to run its own publishing department: even had there been a case for doing so, the investment needed would have been disproportionate to the cost of maintaining the more normal research activity. But between 1983 and 1990 everything necessary gradually became available, in the main as a result of adding increasingly versatile software to standard office equipment, and, as general awareness that there was a new technology to be exploited increased, so it added force to the argument that the social research professions should do more to improve their dissemination activity. No doubt in the wider world the process was more circular–the technological advances were a response to an appetite for information–but the picture inside the social research profession showed a few relatively small, diffuse organisations seizing the practical possibilities of the moment. The 1983 seminar thus set the Dartington Unit in the direction of a pattern of working in which research and development would be theoretically and practically intertwined. Irresistible political forces were at work, but researchers, practitioners and consumers were also being chivvied into a closer relationship by technological change.

Before 1993, any information design and most of the work associated with publishing at Dartington were subcontracted. The evolution of the *Going Home* study suggested there might be advantages in trying to establish a closer relationship between researcher, developer and information designer; then the prospect of the two major projects already mentioned–the widespread implementation of the *Looking After Children* materials and preparation of the 'Blue Book' *Child Protection: Messages from Research*–demanded that the three activities were further enmeshed.

To use a catalogue of technological

development during the 1980s as a way of describing the evolution of a new research enterprise whose principal aim is to improve the services provided for children and families in need will seem a curious choice, but it is an area where technology has played an absolutely vital role: without the personal computer it could not have happened and because of it procedures and relationships inside and between local authorities and research organisations have been revolutionised. To say so is a cliché (as well as a likely exaggeration). Less obvious and less readily understood is the parallel argument that because of what has happened it may no longer be sensible or possible for research scientists to conduct research, for writers to write or for designers to visualise and package the results, all in their self-contained worlds.

The relationship between research and information design will remain an uneasy one nevertheless. The old edifices of the print and publishing industries may have crumbled, but research knowledge continues to be based on conventionally conceived and presented texts. The research text is the result of an extremely exacting, frequently bruising process and, partly for that reason, once finished, it may be regarded as untouchable by its authors. Whoever is responsible for preparing academic writing for publication may suggest ways of presenting the material to better advantage, but is unlikely to want to intrude to the extent of arguing, for example, that certain passages might be done away with altogether, that the whole thing might be shortened by forty per cent or certain chapters replaced by a sequence of

A design note for researchers

The term 'information design', which is discussed in the next Section came to prominence in the graphic design world during more or less the same period. An International Institute of Information Design had its inaugural meeting in 1988 and at its second annual conference in Austria in 1993 agreed the following definition of members' shared concerns: 'Information design is the defining, planning and visualisation of the contents of a message and the environment it is presented in with the intention of achieving particular objectives in relation to the needs of target users.' A British Information Design Association was formed in 1991.

In a study of journal use even thirty years ago, researchers from the American Psychological Association estimated that a sixth of 429 journal articles were read by no-one, and a third by no more than two people. It should not be forgotten either, that the use of writing as a medium for the dissemination of scholarly research and opinion was long regarded as a poor substitute for the egalitarianism of direct verbal communication. Ironically, it has long been suspected that the very proliferation of formal, written channels of communication is one of the chief factors that drives professionals to rely upon informal, oral ones.
See Garvey, W. and Griffith, B. 'Scientific communication; its role in the conduct of research and the creation of knowledge', *American Psychologist* 26, pp349-362, 1971.

annotated diagrams. Ten years ago interference on this scale was in any case out of the question in a publishing field in which editions were small, the market was narrow and the profit extremely marginal. Now the technology permits just this sort of critical interaction between researcher, writer, designer and publisher at every stage in the drafting process. The Dartington Unit regards the change as a great advance; its detractors are likely to regard it as a distraction, a nuisance, or even an adulteration of science.

Furthermore, before plunging on, one must acknowledge the argument that those who conduct research should not worry themselves, even now, with the practicalities of communicating the results, in case their independence is contaminated. It must still be a danger that in the way of all pragmatic dealings with the world, too many allowances will be made and precision and impartiality will be sacrificed. And it is surely not beyond the bounds of possibility that as the world clutters up with information, the value of pure scientific endeavour may actually increase. It may turn out to be a central paradox of the information age, when so much is published indiscriminately in so many forms, that the unscripted lecture given without visual aids retrieves its former, highly influential mystique.

▶ some first attempts: *Going Home*

When the information design experiment began the first edition of *Going Home* was nearly in press. The book included prototypes for a series of checklists which predicted different return outcomes at successive moments in a child's care career.

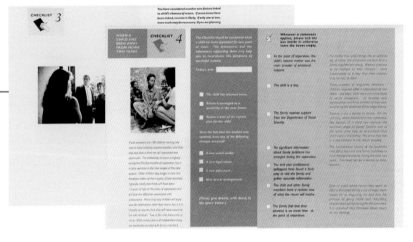

The prototypes were used as the basis for a checklist booklet for social workers already mentioned. The publication was designed in-house on a desktop system and the job presented to the printer as disk files which were run directly to film. The Unit held the stock and distributed it itself. During the next three years several slightly revised printings were issued. Local authority responses to the design and content were used to inform the production of a final revision in 1997/8.

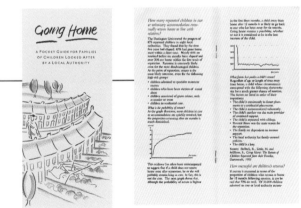

Other later transcriptions of *Going Home* included a parents' guide published in association with Family Rights Group, an eight-page booklet for the Judicial Studies Board, an article for *The Magistrate* and an experimental software package described on page 34.

As the script for *Going Home*, was being prepared, several other exercises were underway. One such 'transitional' piece produced for the Department of Health was *Residential Care: A Review of the Research,* designed and prepared at Dartington, but supplied to HMSO as finished disc files in 1993. At the heart of the book is a series of cross referenced tabulated directories of research material —an attempt to display visually aspects of residential care well served and less well served by research.

Practitioners often telephone the Unit to find out what a certain study says. A deadline will invariably be bearing down on them; there will be no time to read a book. As part of the first wave of translation work, the Unit's major published studies, *After Grace–Teeth* (1975), *Lost In Care* (1986), *Access Disputes in Child Care* (1989), findings from the then continuing study of Youth Treatment Centres published in 1998 as *Secure Treatment Outcomes* and *Going Home* were condensed into 12 or 16 page A5 booklets. At about the same time other more local Unit studies of initiatives in Hampshire and West Devon were translated into 'bookmark' size 210x99mm 12 page booklets. Précis work of this sort is actually rather peripheral to the development process to be described here, but some of the problems that can arise from the severe condensing of research material are discussed.

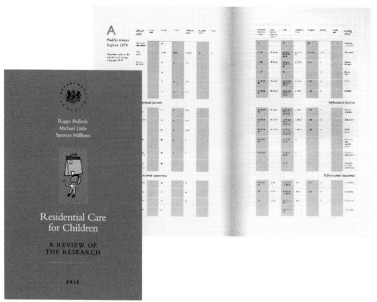

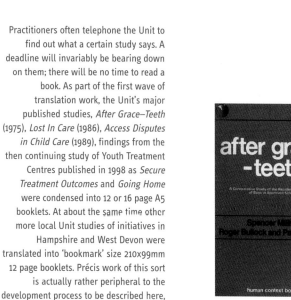

## ▶ some first attempts: *Looking After Children*

At the time of the information design appointment, the *Looking After Children* research project was moving into its development phase. It is one of the ironies of development work in the Unit's narrow field that the final scale of an initiative should sometimes be unpredictable. The *Looking After Children* materials were originally conceived as a way of monitoring the success of state intervention in children's lives. Their usefulness to social work practice was seized upon and the research team was propelled into the business of questionnaire and form design and into a complicated three-cornered relationship involving also HMSO, who laid out and published prototype Assessment and Action Records 1 and subsequently a range of planning review forms. As the in-house information design role became established, so more of the design and production responsibility was offered to Dartington, although HMSO remained the publisher. Revised Planning and Review forms were designed in the winter of 1993; all the forms were remodelled and revised 2 during the following winter for the launch of the national programme in May 1995. Since 1992 the Unit has also been responsible for sub-editing, laying out and seeing into print a project newsletter 3.

1

2

3

Work on the overview of the Department of Health's Child Protection programme began in earnest in 1993. The major part is represented in *Child Protection Messages from Research* which was published in June 1995. There was involvement too in the design of the series of publications known as the *Studies in Child Protection* which emerged from the research programme. All the work was seen through the press in association with HMSO. Dissemination of the policy and practice implications of *Child Protection: Messages from Research* is continuing. The complexities involved in dealing with editorial supervision of different kinds are discussed on pages 43-44.

Between 1992 and 1995, the Unit conducted research at the Caldecott Community in Kent, resulting in the book *A Life Without Problems?* Caldecott provides a secure framework in which children, adolescents and young adults can recover from the setbacks that have blighted their early lives. The research was designed to show to what extent the Community's work benefited the children it looked after. The research report, published by Arena, was unusual for the extent to which it interwove the diaries of a teenage girl living at Caldecott with a more conventional research analysis. That relationship between a personal account and scientific analysis was condensed and remodelled in a secondary A4 pamphlet designed and produced 'in-house'.

## ▶ some first attempts: *Matching Needs and Services*

In 1995 the Unit contributed to the work of the Support Force for Children's Residential Care, which produced a series of publications about preparing, planning and costing services. Out of the relationship emerged the conceptual framework for a method of calculating local authority needs on the basis of an audit of services provided during the previous year. The process was described in *Matching Needs and Services: The Audit and Planning of Provision for Children Looked After by Local Authorities*, which was designed and published 'in-house' in conjunction with the Support Force during the summer of 1995. In the sense that the report and the form of publication were prepared as part and parcel of one conceptual process and put into circulation as a prototype designed to encourage local authorities to conduct their own research, it is the most refined example to date of the Unit's approach to information design—it was also the most hurried.

Just as ten years ago it would not have been sensible for a research organisation of Dartington's size to equip itself with a design suite, so five years ago the global dissemination of research by computer was too vague a notion to contemplate. Even now, a certain uneasiness goes with writing about such things: today's jargon is tomorrow's gibberish. Nevertheless, at the time of writing the Unit has to consider the usefulness of being involved in software development, of posting 'home pages' on the Worldwide Web and exploiting the potential of e-mail and the Internet as research delivery routes. The design of computer software was an issue first in relation to the *Looking After Children* development project, but because the availability of computers among local authorities was and continues to be so variable, progress has been fairly tentative. Translating the materials for local authorities to use interactively on screen has since fallen to a specialist unit at the the University of Bath (SSRADU). For its part the Unit began experimenting in 1994 first with a computer-based equivalent of the *Going Home* checklists to enable a team leader to carry out an audit of long-stay cases and to prevent drift. The prototype included printable summaries and a version of the parents' guide, see page 45. Latest initiatives include building an on-line directory of research in collaboration with Research in Practice and the Centre for Social Policy: Warren House.

## ▶ conclusion: looking for a balance between the 'r' and the 'd'

A note about book publishing

The Dartington Unit's first books *The Hot-house Society* and *The Chance of a Lifetime* were about the English public schools and so were fairly readily accepted by Weidenfeld and Nicolson and Penguin. *After Grace–Teeth*, on the other hand, dealt with the Approved Schools and in marketing terms was about as attractive as a textbook on dentistry; it was three years before a willing specialist publisher, Human Context Books (The Chaucer Press) could be found. Since then, apart from studies which the Department of Health contracted to HMSO before privatisation, Unit book publishing has been in the hands of John Irwin of Ashgate Publishing, whose academic imprints also include Avebury and Arena. There is a question in all this about the most useful relationship between researcher, developer and the publishing industry. *Matching Needs and Services* just described, which was published 'privately' by Dartington in conjunction with the Support Force for Children's Residential Care sold four times as many copies as Avebury will print of a forthcoming book on *Quantitative Methods in Social Policy Research*. That John Irwin has encouraged the Unit and been willing to collaborate in the attempt to improve its development work has been an important contributing factor to any small progress that has been made.

Nearly a decade and a half has passed since the Department of Health and Social Security convened a seminar to discuss the dissemination of child care research. At the time, as far as the Unit was concerned, development work consisted mainly of lectures to professional groups (at the time an unfashionable activity for a serious academic); today probably a fifth of the Unit's time is devoted to what is now called scientific development. Since more research is being produced and much of it is of a higher scientific quality as well as being more applicable to practice, the potential audience is wider and larger than before. In 1983 the idea that health visitors might feel the need to read an overview of social work research or that a student of forensic psychiatry in Kuala Lumpur might browse through a summary of a study on extremely difficult and disturbed adolescents on a laptop computer was inconceivable: most delegates would not have associated health visitors with children in need nor would they have used a computer.

Much orthodox scientific research is conducted at Dartington, whose development still extends no further than a scholarly journal to be read by fewer than a hundred people. There is also additional development work, not described in any detail here—newsletters, conferences for senior managers and summaries of what speakers say. Then, there are the hybrids of research and development like *Going Home* where the 'd' is part of the 'r' proposal and the evaluation of the 'd' constitutes the latest evidence on the experiences of children looked after.

Any progress the Unit may have made in these areas since 1983 has been in the area of making connections between the theory and concepts used to underpin research and those used to design, disseminate and evaluate the developmental products. It would not have been possible had an information designer been far removed from the researchers or had the development process been conceived as an unconnected activity. Whatever there is to show has been the product of a collaboration.

The expansion of development activity implies a concern to find an effective balance between 'r' and 'd'. Some North American academics collect enough free air miles during conference tours for them to travel first class several times round the globe: too much 'd' and not enough 'r'. There is also the need to strike the balance between researcher and developer: the former may seethe when two-fifths of a well-wrought text is cheerfully struck away; the latter must learn to fret about the difference between cause and correlation. The mechanics of the relationship are explored in the next chapter.

# 4 Development, design, dissemination

This chapter tries to illustrate some of the information design questions that may need to be considered if research knowledge is to be presented and used to best effect. It describes how various drafts of research development materials were designed and produced and how a pilot version of the *Going Home* checklists provided a basis for the more extensive experiments described in later chapters.

Wurman, R.S. *Information Anxiety: What to do when information doesn't tell you what you need to know,* Pan, London, 1989

There is a self-approving aspect to the designer's search for a respectable place in the information age. Speaking of the fashion among graphic designers like Saul Wurman and Massimo Vignelli to call themselves 'information architects', the American critic Andrew Blauvelt observes: 'Vignelli... invokes the title of architect to enhance the social standing afforded by such a claim: the undisputed status of a licensed profession with aspirations of planning, order and control. In the light of the social realities of most architectural practice today, Vignelli might have claimed the more appropriate title of "information developer". After all, there is no sphere of pure information or untainted practice that is somehow beyond, or above, the messy realities and compromised complexities of contemporary life.'

Blauvelt, A., 'Unfolding information/ unpacking meaning', Emigré No. 40 *The Info Perplex,* Sacramento, 1996

Design in the context of dissemination is not about surface styling, nor even about the careful presentation of good work. It concerns a modelling process which the American information designer, Saul Wurman, has called 'the construction of explanations'. Wurman applied his definition in particular to the design of city guides in the 1970s. Information designers were to say to themselves: 'Here is a city; people get lost in it; how can I describe the city so that people no longer get lost?'. On first acquaintance the analogy may not seem very useful, since research is so much more abstract in its references and is far removed from everyday practicalities. What counts though is the way the notion of construction illuminates the architectural aspect of the process: a designer assembles tangible objects out of necessary elements.

A second aspect of the analogy is that a designer of maps will want to 'explain' the city in different ways to meet the requirements of different travellers. For a vagrant, a telephone engineer and a gourmet three different but none the less accurate explanations may be constructed; it would be a mistake moreover, to palm off on one client a guide intended for either of the other two. The analogy to map making can be applied to the design process, too. The question, 'How am I to construct an explanation of this city?' invites a number of answers from a variety of media. A folding map showing underground conduit and manholes will help the telephone engineer, a list of restaurant telephone numbers small enough for the breast pocket will be better for the gourmet. The right explanation may require a narrative description, a diagram, and a series of photographs. Depending on what is required, the proportion of one to the rest will vary.

A third factor is especially relevant to the approach to development work the Dartington Unit is seeking to establish: good mapping makes it possible to build better cities—in other words, it can be one of the functions of information design to pinpoint and so remedy the weaknesses of research or, more positively, to identify new possibilities. Whatever theory drives the research drives the development work; the development work informs the research.

Even from such a sketchy description, the identifying characteristics of design applied to the

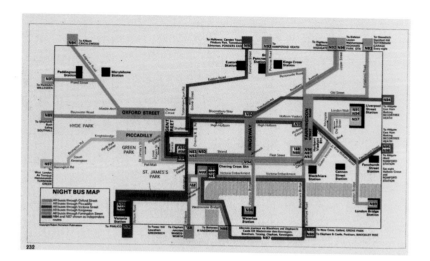

To make the point about the differences between equally accurate representations of the same physical reality, here are maps of central London designed (top) for bus travellers and (bottom) for sightseeing river traffic. From *Nicholson's London Guide*, Robert Nicholson Publications.

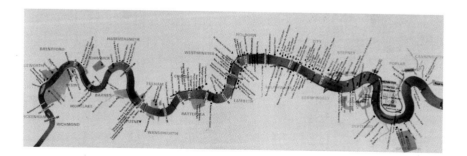

dissemination process begin to emerge. For example:

**1** Information design concerns the construction of explanations; the task of the designer is to determine what form an explanation should take and within that form what materials should be used and how they should be combined.

**2** The materials used to construct an explanation– illustration, text, chart, footnote, photograph–will vary in proportion to one another from object to object, but ought to be considered equally valuable.

**3** The work is to be regarded as a true collaboration. It is not a question of politely acknowledging contributions but of collecting and combining a wide range of creative skills.

Now to take each in turn in more detail:

**1** Few would embark on a project without giving some thought to the product, whether a leaflet, a report, even an exchange of information over the telephone. Under ordinary circumstances, a research organisation is likely to arrange a meeting of researchers to plan the gathering, collating and analysis of material, but is rather less likely to ask along those who will design and assemble the final publishing and dissemination materials. In information design, in mapping the 'city' of a research project, all processes are represented from the outset. Until very recently, though this degree of emphasis on form would have been novel, the result could not have varied far from a narrowly defined norm: the book, the journal article, the summary, the lecture, the radio interview. Desktop technologies have not only extended the range of possibilities for printed

The simple argument against the sovereignty of text hinted at here will probably strike information designers working in the new technologies as woefully timid. The growth of the Internet is refuelling the search for entirely visual languages and rekindling interest for example in the ancient ideographic scripts of the Mixtecs and Aztecs. Timothy Housz, the creator of *The Elephant's Memory* visual writing programme, two examples of which are shown here, regards himself and others in the field as designers searching for new ways to bridge cultures and build transitional spaces between natural languages. Illustrations reproduced from *Intelligent Tutoring Media* Vol. 7 No. 2, 1996

An ideogram showing two actors taking something from one another

'I hear the rabbit on the telephone'

material, but introduced new variants: the Worldwide web page, e-mail and multimedia presentations are obvious examples.

2 Once the principle of conceptual planning has been established much of the remainder will follow, because it introduces the designer not as the solver of problems but as someone who helps to give form to ideas. The idea of the designer as a 'language worker' who formulates documents by arranging, sizing, framing and editing images and texts harks back to the 1920s Bauhaus theories of Kandinsky, Klee and Moholy-Nagy. In their synthetic view, the typographical grids, graphs and diagrams of information graphics were to be regarded as the basis of a comprehensive and comprehensible visual script. In practical terms the approach asks not only 'is the meaning of text A sufficiently clear?' but also 'Do texts A and B arranged with diagrams C and D on pages E and F convey what is wanted? Does arrangement x do the job better than arrangement y? More fundamentally, Is page size A more appropriate, more economical than page size B?'

The corollary of this argument concerns the status of the text. In much research and dissemination work printed text is likely to be the medium most heavily relied upon. Most of what a research unit produces is intended to be read. But it does not necessarily follow that text is the only suitable carrier for findings or messages. In this scheme, text is a negotiable component, likely to be more important than the image but not necessarily so in every case, likely to determine the shape of page or the choice of media but not always; certainly not to be regarded as the near

faultless expression of an individual intelligence.

3 The sort of method being described is bound to be collaborative. At its best it will harness skills from a variety of disciplines–data gatherers and analysts, report writers, illustrators and graphic designers–and combine them with elegance and economy. Again, a good analogy is to be found in architecture, where the method of engagement with the work is by group practice, where the process is driven by ideas about performance and function and where the product is a building in which indispensable contributions–for example those of the structural engineer and the draughtsman–may be entirely hidden.

Another model, useful for the perspective it brings to the business of writing and the 'ownership' of text, is the newspaper office, where stories are commonly written by one hand (the reporter), assessed by another (the news editor), earmarked for a certain page by a third (the chief sub editor) and remodelled by a fourth (a sub editor). In deciding where a particular piece of information belongs, where it will have most impact, a text will pass from hand to hand several times; no-one who processes it will regard it as his or her own. A reporter's name will frequently appear next to a story in which barely a sentence of her original work has survived. It will then find itself surrounded by photographs, graphics, cartoons, advertisements, each one of which will have crossed as many desks, and each will bear upon the meaning conveyed by the whole.

Other factors in the process of newspaper production are as illuminating. Certain sub editors will be chosen to rewrite certain stories into a different style or the reporter concerned may be asked to develop a different angle, to give the text more or less 'drama' or 'spin'. Even a short piece may have been compiled by several hands from many sources. Paradoxically, part of this work will have involved introducing a vital element of consistency to make it seem as if it had been written by an individual sending a letter home.

A picture begins to emerge, then, of research dissemination as a multi-dimensional co-operative process which derives its direction and its momentum from the particular nature of the job in hand, but is driven by the same theory that drives the research. The next task is to show how these principles have begun to be applied.

When ideas about information design were introduced to the process, the *Going Home* checklist material existed in a fairly standard form–in the closing chapters of the report to the Department of Health, later published as *Going Home* which was in the process of being adapted for book publication by Dartmouth (Bullock et al 1993). The checklists required validation. In an effort to combine research and development, it was decided to publish the checklists separately and test their usefulness to field social workers, an exercise that would also check the validity of the factors they contained.

From the outset, various design considerations were fairly clear. For example, it was important that the publication should convey a clear idea of the checklists' purpose: that they were not intended to be the arbiter of a decision whether or not to send a child home, rather that they were designed to help social workers focus on plans, comprehend the wider processes of separation and return and place this understanding in a context of common experience. It would have been an obvious mistake to give the forms the appearance of a tax return, not much better to make them look like a marketing questionnaire in a magazine. It was important that the checklists should represent something of the nature of the research from which the factors had emerged–to demonstrate, for example that it did not rest on anecdote.

At the other extreme, although the statistical analysis of the data had been quite sophisticated, care had to be taken not to alienate a profession that also set store by intuition and empathy. A further requirement was that the material should be presented in an economical and orderly way. If the forms were to function properly as a means of collecting data for further research, social workers had to be encouraged to complete them. The layout therefore needed to be immediately comprehensible, the underpinning evidence needed to be visible and close to its point of reference, but it must not discourage an impatient scanning eye. The finished publication should also represent a fair transaction between the practitioner and the researcher, in which one paid attention and gave information to the other.

Decisions about size and shape were driven by ordinary social work practice: the booklet needed to fit in a filing cabinet; it had to be slight enough to slot easily into the case file concerning a particular child and at the same time distinctive enough not to be lost.

A page from an early, warts-and-all draft of the *Going Home* checklists to show how the work proceeded. Some of the corrections marked on the sheet are to do with straight-forward graphic design problems, some to do with clumsy writing, some to do with the need to distinguish the statistically significant factors the research study had isolated from the more general information gathering exercise.

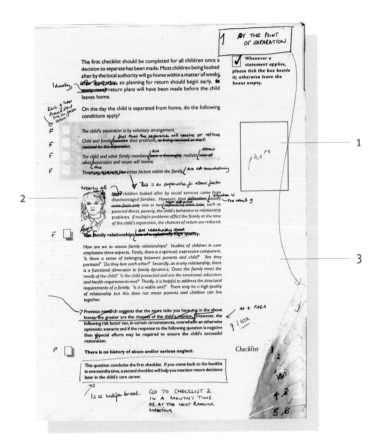

On these criteria the argument for an A4 page format was irresistible. The next task was to classify and then to make visual distinctions between different types of information the checklists were required to convey:

- information given to the individual user about when and how to complete the form
- checklist questions or statements which incorporated predictive factors
- checklist questions or statements which did not incorporate predictive factors
- information to demonstrate the relevance of the checklist questions
- supporting statistical information from the research
- supporting case material from the intensive study which described the process of return as a series of episodes.

There are a number of obvious devices designers use to distinguish between text elements:

- varying the weight, style and size of a typeface or using a number of different typefaces
- applying colour or making use of 'white' space
- choosing a consistent position on a page for certain recurring classes of information
- using headlines and subheads
- using illustrations or photographs and typographical devices, eg boxes and bullets.

In the first mock-up, virtually all the text was left to run in a single broad column and a simple variation between roman **bold** and *italic* fonts from a single typeface **Gill sans** was relied upon to distinguish checklist questions from the supporting anecdotal information. A narrower right-hand column **1** was to be used as a channel for statistical

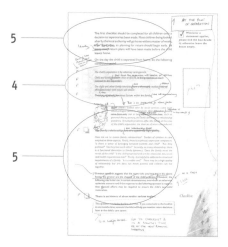

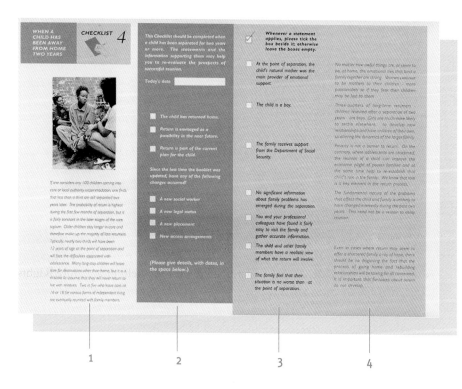

and bibliographical material and there was an intention to introduce icons **2** to distinguish further between the different components. Photographs **3** were to be added to give the pages textural variety and, so it was hoped, a degree of humaneness.

Having completed a prototype, however, the approach shown on the previous page seemed less than ideal, chiefly because the statements social workers were required to check **4** were separated by sizeable blocks of supporting text **5**. This supporting text, though relevant to the process, was not to be regarded as essential reading. In this first try-out, it looked rather as if the social worker was being required to absorb a great deal of background information in order to answer a few ostensibly very simple questions.

Progress was made by turning the page layout through 90 degrees and so working in 'landscape' instead of 'portrait' format. The original two-column arrangement was translated into four and, where the length of a checklist warranted it, the vertical spread was allowed to cross two pages and so become part of a continuous A3 sheet. In this arrangement the first column was used for general information from the research **1**, the second for instructions and general case queries **2**, the third for the checklist questions and statements **3**, the fourth for information intended to illuminate the concerns raised by the checklist **4**. It became possible to work with just three weights of *Gill sans* italic type and to make consistent use of colour: blue for the instruction column and a varying third colour for each of the five checklists.

A principle of the Unit's developing approach to information design is that text should be regarded as a fluid or at least a flexible element. There must be different specialist texts to meet the requirements of different readers. To date, the extracts relating to a particular project have usually been derived from the same master document, which in most instances has been a research report prepared for the Department of Health. In the case of the *Going Home* study this master text has been summarised and reworked for half a dozen different purposes–notably for the checklists, but also for the Family Rights Group guide for families and for an experiment in computer software design. Both these are described below.

The many reservations associated with re-jigging research texts have already been referred to in the context of Jane Rowe's parting advice to the Department of Health. They stem largely from the conviction that the full report will always be a well-wrought summation of a highly intricate process and, consequently, that to shorten or dismantle the contents must weaken or distort the meaning. But there is a distinction to be drawn here between summary writing (shortening), where an attempt is made to represent the gist of the whole on a smaller scale and information design (remodelling), where the requirement is to develop certain particulars for a special purpose. In the case of the *Going Home* checklists the intention was not to produce anything that would make possible on a small scale the gradual accumulation of general insight allowed by deep reading of a complete research report. It was to be another

kind of encounter, in which professionals could extract from the materials whatever inspiration was useful to them in particular situations. Thus simple, even simplistic 'snapshot' statements such as 'there are continuities in the child's life' were illuminated by marginal notes, quoting in this case authorities such as Maluccio, Fein and Olmstead on the relationship between continuities and permanency planning. Another quotation concerned the general relationship between loss of continuity and social isolation among young people. This gradual enlargement of ideas through a group or series of printed particulars, first tested in the checklists, has become a characteristic of the Unit's approach.

Other findings of the *Going Home* report, in particular information about the process of separation and return and its effect on family life, were further reworked in the pocket guide for families of children looked after, produced in collaboration with Family Rights Group. In this case, the formal considerations were less severe: the basic requirement was for something cheap enough for social workers to feel able to give away and attractive enough for a parent to be prepared to receive, which would convey useful messages from the research in simple language without obscuring the complexity of what was being described. The result was a 32-page (one-third A4) booklet drafted with the help of a Family Rights Group researcher and a team of parents with first-hand experience of separation from their children. The approach was more conventionally journalistic: for example, the top margins of the opening pages were used for a series of simple

In her unpublished paper *Some Thoughts on the Department of Health's Research Reviews*, 'pink book' editor Jane Rowe listed these dangers of summary writing.
• Because reference may be made to only one finding from a particular study, there is a risk that this will give a misleading impression of the focus and/or range of that study.
• There is a very real risk that the inevitable condensation of a review and the effort to be clear and strong will result in oversimplification of messages which the researchers themselves have taken pains to qualify.
• Because the messages conveyed in this sort of review are powerful and convincing, there is a correspondingly strong risk that distorted and misleading messages could arise from any bias in the selection and presentation of the material.

positive messages:

- *Parting always hurts, but don't let yourself be defeated by it - there are things you can do to help*
- *It is very likely that your child will come home and that things will work out well*
- *Think of ways to show how much everyone in your family is concerned about your child's future.*

Five of the seven 'episodes' identified in the intensive study were translated into short sections under simplified idiomatic headings:

'The point at which return becomes an issue' became *Getting ready*

'The point at which return occurs' became *The big day*

'The honeymoon' became *Home sweet Home*

'Acrimonious exchanges between family members' became *The row*

'The point at which a new modus vivendi is established' became *Working things out*

Collaborating with outside organisations meant that striking the right note became more of an issue. For example, Family Rights Group were naturally concerned that whatever was published should help the child and his or her family; similarly, the parents who were consulted were anxious that the language should be accessible and speak for their own experience. As a consequence, parents disapproved of the general statement, 'people in social work understand that family life does not have to be easy or particularly comfortable for relationships to be strong' on the grounds that it was not borne out by their unhappier experiences of participation and partnership. Family Rights Group took exception to the use of the word 'honeymoon' to describe the episode immediately following reunion, on the grounds that the connotation with sexual romance was inappropriate.

On the part of the researchers there were worries about the level of hidden propaganda. The omission of key words or phrases in early drafts often had the effect of translating the research finding, 'most children looked after go home' to the more evangelical—and unsubstantiated—claim that 'most children looked after *should* go home'.

To what extent were any of these passing editorial disputes to be regarded as design questions? The rule must be that there will be circumstances in which the page dictates its requirements to the text and others in which the text dictates the requirement to the page. Graphic design tends to the former, conventional academic practice to the latter, but the value of the constructional approach is that one persuasion can give shape to the other. For example, it was an important factor in the design of the *Going Home* booklet that the brief descriptions of episodes of return should begin at the top of a page and end at the foot; similarly, in the preceding section, that each page should be the vehicle for a single manageable idea. Thus the question of whether to extend the discussion about continuities to deal with the problem of private fantasies was in the end as much a question of page layout as research.

In connection with the hope that the practitioner checklists would represent a fair exchange of information between research and practice, a serious shortcoming was that while the information they were designed to collect would be unique in every case, the information they imparted must always be the same. A remedy, not seriously entertained, would have been to print perhaps half a dozen variants in which different selections of research material were used in the marginal notes. The benefit to the practitioner completing his or her tenth identical checklist would then have been one of periodic and unexpected refreshment; the questions would be the same but the sidelights on the issues would be different.

On the face of it, computer software (especially on-line versions made available via the World Wide Web that are rather beyond the scope of this account) make more spontaneous interaction between practitioner and research eminently possible. Software design was an issue first in relation to *Looking After Children* but has been largely confined to the collection of statistical information. Development of *Going Home* created an opportunity to experiment more freely. The checklists were simplified and re-assembled to connect with selections from the research literature. Designed with team leaders in mind, the package seemed to begin to offer a means of applying best knowledge about separation, drift and return directly to casework. A key aspect of the programming was to use 'digital publishing' technology, which makes it possible to connect and interweave any number of library documents and also to present them in a printable form. Thus, to take the marginal notes in the *Going Home* checklist publication as an example, re-translated from paper to the screen they can be used as openings to libraries of much more detailed, precisely catalogued reference material. As the side

diagram shows, information design for the computer screen–for CD-ROM or the Internet–is able to model a conceptual approach in which casework particulars are informed by a stream of relevant evidence. Alas, work so tentatively undertaken between 1994 and 1996 begins to look out-of-date as this book goes to press in 1998.

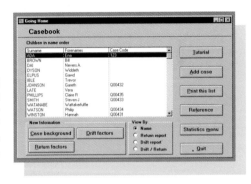

From 1995 onwards digital publishing technology made it possible to create direct links between a *Going Home*-based checklist database and files of printable information from the research literature.

# 5 Measuring dissemination

In this chapter different approaches to the thorny problem of measuring the effectiveness of research dissemination are discussed. The concept of three levels of usefulness– immediate, intermediate and ultimate–is explained.

Which have been the most successful and which the least successful of the projects Dartington has undertaken? Spencer Millham has little doubt concerning the relative impact of the Unit's studies of boarding schools and of secure units. The boarding school studies, he says

'had no influence whatsoever. Quite probably the research was commissioned to have very little influence, to pacify the Left or to imply action in an area where none was intended… (it) was a good example of cosmetic research'

As far as the secure unit studies were concerned

'…the Department of Health could not have moved more swiftly … we found ourselves in a grand London hotel addressing hundreds of the great and the good … the money for an extension of security was promptly cut off'

On reflection, however, Millham acknowledges the inadequacies of such superficial judgements. The outcome of a research programme is no easier to assess than the outcome of any other modification of a complex social system. Firstly, as Parker and colleagues found in a different context, the verdict from any such assessment is likely to depend to a large extent on the moment when it is undertaken. Research may take a long time to infiltrate thinking so completely that it becomes recognisable as 'knowledge'. Some research dazzles briefly and quickly fizzles out, other ideas smoulder for years before igniting. Even then, acceptance into the canon of knowledge is never more than provisional. Knowledge advances as much by elimination as by accumulation, and yesterday's ideas are continually re-evaluated in the light of today's. The influence of a work such as Hayek's *Road to Serfdom* or *The Thoughts of Chairman Mao* would certainly have been assessed differently in 1990 as compared to 1970. No doubt both will be seen in a new light a decade hence.

Any assessment of outcome is likely to depend not just upon *when* but upon *how* success is measured. It is one thing to change a policy or to issue a new set of guidelines, quite another to change practice. The Unit's studies of the approved schools provide ample evidence that administrative responsibilities are more easily changed than professional cultures, and both common sense and the laws of thermodynamics suggest that the easier a change is to accomplish, the easier it will prove to reverse.

In charting the rise and fall of ideas, moreover, the history of knowledge cannot easily be separated from the history of the institutions that create knowledge. It is not hard to understand why the status of knowledge in the social sciences, and the role of that knowledge in altering or maintaining social and economic systems, has proved to be sociology's equivalent of the Somme, in which hundreds of thousands of words are expended in pursuit of the tiniest concession by the other side.

★　　　★　　　★

With these cautions in mind, it is necessary to decide what to measure and then when to measure it. To take the former first, Knott and Wildavsky (1981) differentiate 'seven standards of utilisation', summarised to the left. By their analysis different Dartington studies would score higher or lower depending upon the standard selected. If 'reception' is regarded as the be-all-and-end-all of dissemination, then a simple tally of the print-runs of various reports illustrated over the page would seriously question Millham's view that early works such as *The Hothouse Society* (60,000 copies) were less influential than studies such as *Locking Up Children*, of which only 2,500 copies saw daylight.

However, quantity is no substitute for quality. Cognition might be measured at least within the academic community, by some form of citation analysis. On such criteria, the boarding school studies would again score poorly, whilst a work such as *Lost in Care*, which was purchased by fewer than 3,000 people would be regarded as highly influential. Merely citing a text, however, hardly

proves that an author has read it. How many economists have actually read *The Wealth of Nations*, let alone *Das Kapital*?

At the opposite end of Knott and Wildavsky's scale, consideration of the adoption and implementation of research produces a different balance sheet. The boarding school studies may have had no immediate effect on government policy, but they were very widely discussed in the national media, to the extent of being mentioned in a *Times* leader and serialised in a Sunday broadsheet. So in the short term, the evidence was very definitely received, if not adopted.

Furthermore, the studies were part of a chorus of criticism that was at least partly responsible for the liberalisation of the public schools over the past generation—the almost universal drive towards co-education, for example, and the increasing age at which pupils are first introduced to boarding. By contrast, the fate of the Dartington Unit's own assessment of the implementation of the DHSS Code of Practice that followed *Lost in Care* was that in most cases a copy languished at the bottom of the team leader's drawer or, like the fire drill notice, it was pinned to the board in the social services department. But since the mid-1980s when this assessment was made, times have changed again. New duties placed on local authorities in the *Children Act, 1989* to encourage contact between looked after children and their families have ensured that the recommendations of the *Lost in Care* studies have indeed been implemented in local offices and when court decisions are made.

What of Knott and Wildavsky's final criterion?

---

**'Seven standards of utilisation'**

1 reception
   utilisation takes place when policy makers or advisors receive policy-relevant information

2 cognition
   the policy maker must read, digest and understand the studies

3 reference
   utilisation somehow must change the way the policy maker sees the world

4 effort
   information must influence the actions of policy makers, even if political forces or other events block their efforts

5 adoption
   it is essential that information goes on to influence policy outcomes

6 implementation
   adoption without implementation is a hollow victory

7 impact
   only when policy stimulated by information yields tangible benefits to the citizens has utilisation taken place.

Adapted from Knott, J. and Wildavsky, A. 'If dissemination is the solution, what is the problem?' in Rich R. (ed.), *The Knowledge Cycle*, Sage, Beverly Hills, 1981.

Inexperienced academic writers may dwell on the relative merits of different publishers and, in weaker moments, imagine themselves called one day to a book signing session. The reality is likely to be very different. First, the print-runs of academic books are short, indicating that publishers understand the market rather better than authors. Second, because of the way books are marketed these days, many outside the mainstream never even see inside a bookshop.

The following estimates of the print-runs for various Dartington Unit publications give an idea of the narrowness of the readership for scholarly books. They are also a testimony to the service that academic publishing houses and, in a different way, the Department of Health provide. Without them, much of what is written inside universities would be condemned to the 'stack' of the university library.

| Publication | Publisher | Print-run |
| --- | --- | --- |
| Hothouse Society | Weidenfeld/Penguin | 60,000 |
| After Grace—Teeth | Human Context | 3,200 |
| Locking up Children | Saxon-House | 2,500 |
| Lost in Care | Gower | 3,000 |
| Going Home | Dartmouth | 2,000 |
| Child Protection: Messages from Research | HMSO | 40,000 |
| Looking After Children forms | HMSO | 200,000 |
| A Life Without Problems? | Arena | 3,000 |
| Quantitative methods | Avebury | 500 |
| Going Home checklists | In-house | 5,000 |
| Unit newsletters | In-house | 2,500 |
| Conference brochures | In-house | 4,000 |

What unequivocal evidence of 'tangible benefits to the citizens' can be produced to justify expenditure on scientific research development? Determining whether any initiative has had any noticeable impact on client outcomes is far from straightforward, and ethical, logistical, methodological and political problems ensure that it is rarely done. Where inputs can be regulated (for example through random allocation), control and experimental groups can be compared, but such techniques are inevitably better at assessing the effects of entire interventions than in apportioning credit or blame to their individual components. One might count the effectiveness of a political campaign, for example, in votes, but how might one measure the outcome of a particular leaflet, a news item, a speech or a conversation?

Even having unequivocally identified change, it must then be assessed for better or worse. In manufacturing, simply counting the number of units sold before and after will give a reasonable idea of the effectiveness of a promotional campaign. A positive outcome is harder to quantify when the objective is the overall welfare of children and families. Social work interventions such as child protection investigations can rarely be considered good or bad in themselves: the question is whether they are appropriate in the circumstances. And supposing they can be said to be for the better, the improvement has still to be shown to be attributable to the intervention under consideration. If prospective mothers in 1997 are deliberately increasing their intake of folic acid, it seems reasonable that the recent Department of Health campaign should take much of the credit, there having been very few other obvious direct influences on folic acid intake in pregnancy. The extent to which the decline in smoking over the past 20 years can be attributed to similar health education campaigns, on the other hand, is less clear, since there have been many influences on smokers, from changing social mores to higher tobacco taxes and anti-smoking legislation. Social work decisions are likewise likely to be influenced by a wide range of factors above and beyond programmes of research dissemination.

If nothing else, such observations show that the evaluation of research dissemination is a complex and controversial business. The four chapters that follow describe various ways in which the task has been attempted by the Dartington Unit over the past three years. To make such an evaluation meaningful, it is necessary to condense Knott and Wildavsky's seven standards of utilisation into a more manageable three. These will be referred to as 'levels of outcome', and each requires a different methodology.

An objection to the scheme proposed by Knott and Wildavsky is that their categories, whilst no doubt very important to a phenomenologist or philosopher of artificial intelligence, are not much help empirically. How can we know experimentally whether someone's opinions have been changed by what they have read? Does the fact that they have read something imply that they have understood it? The answer may be to pay attention to different levels of outcome, in other words to the consequences within an

organisational hierarchy. In those conditions outcomes are distinctive not in terms of the quality of the knowledge within an individual consciousness, but in relation to the status in the organisation of the individual making the assessment.

What does such a scheme look like in practice? Firstly, there are the *immediate* outcomes–the basic question of involvement and uptake. Do those at whom the books are aimed read them, complete the schedules, watch the videos, attend the training days? It might be assumed that some degree of involvement at this level will be a *sine qua non* of any potential benefit that might ensue. These immediate outcomes, like the total sales of a chocolate bar, can be fairly easily measured by the disseminators themselves, without reference to any other party. Gibbons and Tunstill (op cit), for example, use this level of outcome as a simple empirical means of assessing success in dissemination. Newspapers, similarly, seek to impress potential advertisers with circulation figures. Such techniques–more or less equivalent to Knott and Wildavsky's 'reception' standard–have many advantages. They are comparatively quick and cheap to undertake, easily understood and subject to straightforward verification by a third party.

Nonetheless, purchase of a newspaper, or attendance at a training day, is no guarantee that anything is gained from the experience (Gibb, 1992). The *intermediate* level is the one most commonly used within the personal social services. How do people feel about their involvement? What do they think they have gained? Was it relevant to the problems and issues that confront them from day to day? Are they better informed? Do they feel more confident? Or has it left them bemused, even resentful? The establishment of feedback systems to monitor clients' experiences has been mandatory in many contexts since the *Children Act, 1989*. In a similar fashion, anyone who attends a talk or reads a magazine in the 1990s is invariably exhorted to give a reasoned critique of the experience by the organisers or publishers. Again, such outcomes can be fairly easily measured: provided responses can be taken at face value, it is necessary only to ask.

When asked, people may not, of course, tell the 'truth'. Social workers may claim to have read articles they have not, or they may be hesitant to admit that they read books at all in a profession for which the distinction between theory and practice wisdom is often regarded as 'a choice between two different forms of knowing' (Paley 1984). They may lie and they may be mistaken: more likely their untruths will fall somewhere in between. Professionals may lie to protect their own interests or to make academics feel better about themselves; nonetheless, the fact that answers cannot be taken at face value does not mean that they can not be taken seriously. The intermediate level is equivalent to condensing Knott and Wildavsky's five middle standards into one.

The third, and far and away the most difficult and controversial class of outcome measurements, consists of *ultimate* outcomes; what Knott and Wildavsky call 'impact'. Ultimate outcomes reflect the medium-term experiences of the children and families for whom services are designed. Does research development and dissemination increase the sum of human understanding? By how much? The methodological and theoretical questions surrounding such questions are immense.

Clearly, no single methodology can answer questions at each of these three levels. The *Looking After Children* study has, to date, focused primarily on uptake and gained valuable insight into the benefits the materials brought to social work practice. At some point or other, nearly all the developments described in this study have been exposed to evaluation at one of the levels just described. *Going Home* is rather unusual because an assessment of benefit was built into the original research design and all three types of outcome were measured. It combined a number of approaches and techniques.

## Development of materials

The development of the materials was itself a highly experimental process, involving frequent evaluation by a number of different groups.

## Selection of sample

Nine local authorities (or parts of local authorities) were selected to participate in one or other aspect of the exercise. Some were eager, others required persuasion. In some local authorities, the decision was taken at the level of area teams, with the result that some areas preferred not to participate. In other authorities, the decision was taken by the director or his or her assistant.

## Training

Social workers in all the participating areas underwent some form of training in the use of the materials. The nature of this training was deliberately varied, with some areas receiving a very intensive input at area team level over a long period (see Chapter Nine) and others a much less ambitious programme.

## Implementation of materials

All social workers who attended the training sessions were asked to complete a *Going Home* booklet for every child separated from relatives to commence a fresh episode of being looked after over a six month period. They were asked to keep this record in the child's file, updating the information as required, until the child returned home.

## Monitoring

During the six months, the area teams were visited by researchers. Professionals were asked for their impressions of the project, as well as any other observations they wanted to make about the relationships between research and practice, in semi-structured group discussions. At the end of these, a confidential questionnaire was used to collect similar information in a more quantitative manner. This exercise produced 163 completed questionnaires. Since all professionals with direct case responsibility who were present in the office at the time were asked to complete a questionnaire, this means of information gathering is far more reliable than the traditional postal survey. Important individuals, such as team leaders and trainers, were also interviewed individually.

## Collection of data

Some two years after the end of the six-month trial, members of the research team collected booklets from the relevant files, and sought information to fill in any gaps. Booklets were begun by case-workers for 230 children but this represented only half the sample, requiring researchers to organise their completion for a further 233 children. The booklets were removed from the file for analysis once a child had been looked after for two years without returning home, or as soon as a child returned home. Those children who returned home were followed up a year after their reunion to gauge the success of the return. The three levels of outcomes discussed, and the appropriate methodologies to explore each one, are schematised in the table on the next page.

## Results

The results of these activities are at the centre of this study. The design and build evaluations have been described in previous chapters. Since this is a continuing procedure in which one innovation is rapidly succeeded by the next, the process is more important than the results at any one time.

Chapter Six uses an *immediate* level of outcome—the proportion of booklets completed—to compare the success of the project in different local authorities, and to assess what combinations of factors predispose a programme of research development to success or failure. Chapter Seven extends this analysis to include questions of both *intermediate* and *ultimate* outcomes. At the intermediate level, the professionals involved submit their own impressions of the project. At the ultimate level, an attempt is made to assess the 'impact' of the project on the lives of children and families.

Chapter Eight is concerned with professionals' own view of the dissemination process, and thus renews the interest in *intermediate* outcomes. The main results of the survey are presented in an effort to chart the progress of ideas and information from 'cognition' to 'implementation'. Chapter Nine seeks to amalgamate all three levels of outcome measurement, in order to explore the relationships between them. Two very different approaches to research dissemination are compared, contrasted and evaluated on a number of different criteria.

## Three levels of outcome

| Level | What measured | Basic technique | Outcomes assessed by | Strengths and weaknesses |
|---|---|---|---|---|
| Immediate | Availability of research | audit | disseminators | Cheap and easy to quantify. Fairly meaningless |
| Intermediate | Use of research | self-report questionnaire | users | Permits more sophisticated analysis, but relies on self-report |
| Ultimate | Effects of dissemination | multi-variate analysis/randomised controlled trial | auditors | Potentially very useful but requires complex research designs |

# 6 The local context for research development

This chapter tries to assemble some lessons from the successes
and failures among Dartington's research developments by
discussing them in the context of perhaps the most succinct
theory of dissemination in literature, the parable of the sower.
The main conclusions are drawn from the *Going Home* exercise,
but data are also introduced from other initiatives where they
add to the argument.

Eccles, T. *Succeeding with Change: Implementing action-driven strategies*, McGraw Hill, London, 1996

Sunday School children will need no reminding
that in the parable of the sower a proportion of the
seed cast by the farmer falls on hard ground,
where it fails to germinate. Some falls on rocky
ground, where the roots it puts down are too weak
to sustain the young shoots through a heat-wave.
Some falls among the weeds and is choked. Only a
small proportion finds good soil and produces a
healthy crop.

In the scriptural context, the seed's failure to
germinate is attributed to the qualities of the soil.
Organisation theorists similarly have tended to
stress the importance of ground conditions in
determining the fate of dissemination and policy
initiatives. Some authors, particularly within the
business studies literature, see organisations in
terms of wider cultures and suggest that the scope
for increasing yields is limited.

Where the parable is treated as an analogy for
the attempt to disseminate research development,
another hypothesis can be entertained: perhaps the
quality of the seed is at fault. Gibbons and Tunstill
and others have stressed that the professional
response to an initiative is as likely to be a
reflection of the value of the initiative itself as the
quality of the organisational context. However
tempting, it is hardly fair to blame organisational
inertia for failure to make an impact. To a theorist
of business management such as Eccles, for
example,

> when the need for implementation arrives ... one
> can only repeat that old joke that 'if I were you,
> I wouldn't start from here' and then get on with
> the changes irrespective of the starting position

To set 'seed' and 'soil' in opposition, however, is
clearly a mistake, too. It is the interaction of the
two that will determine if a programme of
dissemination thrives or withers, taking also into
account a third factor, the efficiency of the sower,
who may be wasteful or careless and likely to
benefit from more advanced machinery and more
systematic knowledge about inputs and outputs.

One way to gauge the success of the
dissemination aspect of the *Going Home* project is
simply to discover the proportion of checklist
booklets completed, making an assessment of the
kind discussed at the immediate level on page 53.
This is undoubtedly a crude measure, but it has the
advantage of being simple, straightforward and
quantitative.

The checklists were tested in nine local authorities selected to be broadly representative of England and Wales. The first eight used the booklets in a routine way (one was unable to sustain its involvement). The ninth, Midlands County, was involved in a carefully designed experiment, the results of which are described in Chapter Nine. The table below gives the ONS family classification and the number of children looked after in 1994 for each of the nine authorities. It will be noted that the nine selected authorities in combination accounted for about 12% of all children who begin to be looked after within a three month period in England and Wales.

Most took the tools blind. In some cases, it was explained to an assistant director or principal officer in the social services department how the checklists should be used and then they were asked to introduce them to area teams. In others, a training day was offered as a reward for participation but the approach was hardly

systematic. In two authorities the Unit made more intensive training efforts and the results of these are described in Chapter Nine.

Checklists were completed by caseworkers for about half the children separated in the period, but there was much variation. The local authority that contributed the largest number of children to the study was also one with a low 'success' rate; social workers completed a booklet for only a quarter of those separated. In another area, the enthusiasm of management for the project was not matched in area teams and no booklets were completed at all. This authority reluctantly withdrew from the research. Several other authorities, in contrast, achieved a completion rate of around two thirds and some individual teams managed to complete a booklet for everyone. How can these varying responses be explained?

In the parable, a proportion of the seed fails to germinate because the ground on which it falls is barren. Certain contexts simply do not augur well for research development projects. Where

| Local authority | ONS classification[1] | Children looked after during 1995[2] |
|---|---|---|
| Northern Met. | Mining and industrial | 175 |
| Southern mixed county | Urban, mature and rural | 779 |
| London borough | Inner London | 130 |
| Eastern county | Prospering, urban and mature | 1229 |
| North-east Met. | Mining and industrial | 288 |
| Southern rural county | Rural | 335 |
| Welsh county | Mining and industrial | 374* |
| North-west Met. | Mining, industrial and rural | 198 |
| Midlands county | Rural, urban and industrial | 430 |

[1] Source: Wallace, M. and Denham, C., (1996), The ONS Classification of local and health authorities of Great Britain, London, HMSO.
[2] Source: Department of Health and Welsh Office annual statistics on children looked after.
*1993-1994 figures for Welsh County.

relationships (whether between central management and area offices or between employers and trades unions) are tense and suspicious, a project such as *Going Home* may find itself used as political tumble-weed. This does not happen often but it is highly disruptive when it does. Arrangements between the Unit and senior management were boycotted by front-line staff on two occasions. In one area, the project was treated as if it was part of a plan to extend central control over what had hitherto been fairly autonomous areas. In one part of another authority, severe resource constraints and a freezing of staff recruitment caused professionals to resist the project, explicitly on the grounds of the extra work involved but also, according to the coffee room chat, because it was suspected of being a cost-cutting device. The trade union became involved and, although all ended amicably, it was by then too late to complete the project within the time-scale.

In a third area, social workers completed the booklets but expressed reservations about the ideological slant of the materials. They felt that the researchers' initial presentations encouraged social workers to view a return to parents as a positive outcome, irrespective of the family situation. (This pointed to a serious failing in the Unit's presentation skills.) Overall, three groups of practitioners resisted the project, but they did so on very different grounds. Others were more welcoming and were sceptical about the counter-proposition, saying that talk about extending control, cutting costs or pushing a particular ideology reflected the problems facing social

workers at the time.

These findings indicate that research development does not take place in isolation. Previous research has shown how the existing relationships between practitioners and evidence are an important influence on their use of development tools. When social workers pick up an instrument like *Going Home*, they ask a range of questions, not only–maybe not at all–the one that most interests researchers, namely, will this project improve outcomes for children and families?

Other responses were, on the face of it, still more paradoxical. For example, morale in each of the participating authorities was assessed: where it was high, enthusiasm for the *Going Home* materials was lower. The background charac-teristics of those asked to use the instruments were assessed: authorities with younger and more recently qualified social workers completed proportionally more booklets than authorities with an older and more experienced workforce. This finding seems to stand in the face of a body of evidence about the benefits of experience for work with children in need, or it may be that rather than directly rejecting research messages, practitioners may simply ignore them as being statements of the obvious. This response may be more common than researchers would like to imagine; after all, good social research is often only the mirror of good practice.

A fraction of the seeds cast by the sower in the parable landed on rocky ground. They germinated but were unable to put down deep roots so that the tender shoots withered in the midday sun. 'Roots' here are a good metaphor for the chain of command concerned in research development and dissemination. The importance of middle managers who act as a bridge between the vision and ideals of those at the top of an organisation and the different expectations of those who work directly with families is often noted. With *Going Home, Looking After Children* and, more recently, *Matching Needs and Services,* it has been found that the commitment, endurance and insight of the individual given the role of co-ordinating the project, of standing between the authority and external influences, are important variables. In cases where this individual moves jobs, retires or goes on sick leave, the initiative is often left in the hands of local managers who, because of their number and status, are more difficult to enthuse and less likely to influence others. Implementation is seldom something that can be successfully delegated.

Several authorities in the *Going Home* study also underwent substantial reorganisations during the project, changing the boundaries and responsibilities of district teams. Such upheavals have long been recognised as being unhelpful to children looked after: their effect on programmes of research development can be equally damaging. There was an instructive example of 'research drift' when halfway through the project the replacement for one of the original co-ordinators wrote to say she had found a collection of the *Going Home* materials at the bottom of her predecessor's store cupboard; what did we want done with them? Burnes (1992) identifies 'consistent, competent and stable management' as a

Munro, J. 'Facing The Facts', Health Service Journal, October 5th 1995, pp26-27

key asset in the management of change, but it is difficult to sustain in the midst of turmoil.

No matter how stable the communication chain, optimum results are more likely to be achieved if it is short. The sheer size of an authority, expressed in population or acreage, was a major factor determining the success or otherwise of the project. There was a negative correlation ($r = -0.6$, $p < .01$) between the proportion of booklets completed and the number of children separated in each local authority over the period. Larger authorities tended to complete proportionately fewer booklets than smaller ones. A remedy was to target smaller divisions within the bigger social services departments. Consequently, completion rates were poorest when the project attempted to cover a large authority in its entirety and best where the project area was small and geographically compact–either a small authority or part of a larger one.

In the parable, a proportion of the seed failed because the young shoots were choked by thorns. Here the analogy is with the number of separations per team which was negatively correlated ($p<0.05$) with the proportion of booklets completed. In many respects, this is an encouraging finding, since it shows that local authorities which only completed a comparatively small *proportion* of booklets usually completed a reasonable *number*. Nonetheless, booklets were more likely to be completed in quiet rural offices than by urban out-of-hours teams. Munro likewise notes the greater difficulties of reaching the busy GP, compared to the hospital based specialist.

There was a similar, negative correlation

between the completion rate and the rate of children looked after (the greater the proportion separated, the fewer booklets used) but a positive correlation with the ratio of social workers to children within the authority. Professionals acknowledged in interviews that booklets were completed only to the extent that there were few other pressing demands on their time. A clear illustration of such prioritisation is that children removed from home under emergency protection orders were considerably less likely to have a booklet completed than those accommodated under Section 20 of the *Children Act, 1989.* Where a child was placed for adoption, professionals almost always started a booklet, although it rarely predicted a rapid return home.

A similar pattern can be observed in the use of the booklets over time. For nearly three-quarters of children looked after in February at the start of the project, a booklet was completed, compared with only two-fifths in July, towards the end. Thus an element of 'research fatigue' became evident as the number of children looked after began to mount up. The time needed to complete a booklet remained fairly constant, but, as far as those completing the booklets were concerned, the benefits declined as the research material they contained became more familiar.

★      ★      ★

One aim of the *Going Home* developmental project was to evaluate the strengths and weaknesses of various models of research development and so the project was organised differently in each authority. The least intensive model comprised little more than a meeting of researchers with district officers and other middle managers who made a vague commitment to participate. This initiative subsequently came to nothing. The most intensive involved monthly visits from a professor of social work and is described in detail in Chapter Nine. As a rule, the more intensive the approach, the higher the completion rate, but there were exceptions. In the Southern rural county, for example, where there was an intensive input that would not be economically viable in anything but a pilot project, about half (53%) of the booklets were completed, just above the norm (47%). In Northern Met., on the other hand, despite fairly irregular visits by the researchers, the proportion of booklets completed was 64%. The intensity of the research input seemed to be related to personnel factors within the research team. Results were better where one member of the team saw the entire process through (from the initial overtures via training to the collection of data) than when responsibilities were shared or swapped from one member to another midway. This finding also reflects the experience of those seeking to develop the *Looking After Children* and *Matching Needs and Services* materials.

Irrespective of the intensiveness of the approach, the length of the chains of communication involved played a major role in the success of the project. Where researchers were in direct contact with district managers, bypassing central management, results were better than where a central headquarters formed an additional link in the chain. Where social workers had

The factors described here can be illustrated with reference to the best and worst 'performers', in terms of the completion of booklets. Southern-mixed county, the best performer, is a large Shire comprising urban, rural and mature suburban communities. Eight local teams in one division volunteered to participate and contact between the team leaders and the researchers bypassed central management. Training was conducted within the teams rather than centrally and each team was visited in the middle of the research. Although the division was re-organised during the study period, the personnel involved remained much the same. One team failed to complete the exercise when the manager moved elsewhere. In the others, despite the cynicism of some more experienced staff, three-quarters of booklets were completed.

In North-east Met., by contrast, a large metropolitan authority with high levels of deprivation and rates of children looked after, some 60% higher than in Southern-mixed county, no booklets were completed. The project was organised via the Director through the training department and a single training day was rather hurriedly organised and poorly attended. Local teams, whose relations with central management were already strained, balked at the extra work imposed on them without consultation and the project joined a growing list of central management initiatives not implemented at local level. The local co-ordinator went on extended sick-leave at the start of the project, which never really got off the ground

## Conditions and strategies associated with effective research development

|  | Best | Worst |
| --- | --- | --- |
| Size of project area | small | large, |
| Time-scale | short | long |
| Resourcing factors | staff with more time | over-stretched staff |
| Personnel factors | stable, committed | unstable, uncommitted |
| Political factors | management seen as supportive | management seen as hostile |
| Social worker factors | younger, less confident | older, more confident |
| Chain of command | short | long |
| Intensity of input | greater | less |
| Ownership factors | workers choose to participate | workers told to participate |
| Chances of success | very good | very poor |

queries regarding the materials or where the initial prediction of the quantity of materials required proved conservative, the problem was more likely to be speedily resolved where district managers were in direct contact with the Research Unit. In some authorities poor relationships or poor communications between key individuals led to a general loss of momentum and occasionally to a complete breakdown. The original plan in some local authorities involved the collection of all booklets at a central point to ensure ease of collection, but nowhere did this actually prove possible. The more people involved in the co-ordination of the project, moreover, the more likely it was that at least one of them would leave their post.

A final factor influencing the completion rate involved the ownership of the project at local level. According to Eccles (p.55), 'the key variable of implementation is that of obtaining sufficient endorsement for the strategic change'. In some areas, the decision to participate was taken by central management with little staff consultation, and in such circumstances the results were generally disappointing. In others, the research team were originally rather sceptical about the exhaustive steps taken to ensure that participation was based upon a consensus amongst staff but here commitment to the project turned out to be high and the results encouraging.

Fewer than half the *Going Home* booklets issued to social workers were completed by them. Is this finding a cause for optimism or alarm? In the context of the evidence to be presented in Chapter Eight on the amount social work professionals read

Since the strategies adopted and the authorities participating in the *Going Home* project were deliberately varied, the sample of nine authorities was not large enough to permit control for all variables in order to examine the influence of others. The table below summarises both 'soil' and 'seed' factors for the eight authorities most involved. A '+' sign indicates the presence of a factor more favourable to successful research development work, as identified in the preceding text. A '-' sign denotes a less favourable situation. The table also provides details of the proportion of booklets completed: a simple but important measure of the success of the dissemination of the materials.

Overall, there is a high correlation between the proportion of booklets completed and a simple count of auspicious factors (r=0.96, p<0.001). Moreover, whilst the comparative importance of the factors is likely to differ from one developmental initiative to another, it is interesting to note that similar factors have been suggested as important in other programmes of work, such as *Looking After Children* (Ward, 1995). The following table summarises the best and worst contexts for research development exercises.

Factors influencing the use of the *Going Home* materials

| | Welsh | S.Mixed | N. Met. | E.Co. | S. Rural | NE. Met. | N.W.Met. | London Bo. |
|---|---|---|---|---|---|---|---|---|
| A Political resistance | + | + | + | + | + | - | + | + |
| B SW factors | - | - | + | + | - | N K | + | + |
| C Personnel | - | + | + | + | + | - | + | + |
| D Size of authority | - | + | + | - | - | - | + | + |
| E Workload | - | + | + | - | - | - | + | + |
| F Intensity | - | + | - | - | + | - | - | + |
| G Chain of command | - | + | - | - | + | - | - | + |
| H Choice | - | + | - | + | + | - | - | + |
| Total score out of a possible 8 | 1 | 7 | 5 | 4 | 5 | 0 | 5 | 8 |
| % of booklets started | 23 | 68 | 64 | 48 | 53 | 0 | 56 | 66 |

or use research (or other sources like government guidance for that matter) the results are encouraging. Many more social workers have read the research summarised in the booklets than will have read the book and most will have applied the results to at least one case. But set against the seriousness of the issue, that of returning home a vulnerable child, the results could be regarded as depressing. It takes less than 20 minutes to use the *Going Home* instrument, yet only 46% found it necessary to do so.

A more encouraging picture emerges from the recent audit of local authorities using the *Looking After Children* materials. The same range of usage, from low to high was found, but the materials, which take much longer to use than *Going Home* are now embedded in good social work practice.

The findings in this section will not surprise managers familiar with the principles of good implementation, but they may be new to researchers and advocates of research who imagine that more dissemination is a sufficient condition for success. Whether the product be the Blue Book or the Pink Book, a single research project or a DH circular, it is continuity and focus of implementation that make the difference. One shot is not enough. The results are also a reminder that a dissemination strategy is best adapted to the particular needs of the target local authority.

Getting research materials into use, however, covers only the first of Knott and Wildavsky's 'standards of utilisation'–*reception*. Once research is in use, it is necessary to ask further questions - does it influence practice? does it provide any 'tangible benefits to children and families'?

# 7 What difference did *Going Home* make?

This chapter attempts to evaluate how far developmental exercises can make a difference to what social workers do. The primary test is once again the *Going Home* materials. Later, the bigger question of whether any change in practice can be shown to benefit children and families is considered.

A year after the *Going Home* project began, professionals were asked their opinion of it. Most who had completed a checklist booklet said it was useful in the case to which it had been applied and that they knew more about separation and return as a result. This in itself was an achievement. A recognition that nine out of ten looked after children eventually go home, whether professionals like it or not, tends to engender a distinctive view of the social work task.

The pattern of behaviour which suggests that professionals slowly assimilate the developments of research without openly embracing them is reflected in other areas. The audit of local authorities using the *Looking After Children* materials shows that most professionals are willing to accept that the instruments have a vital role to play in planning for children in care or accommodation but that, nevertheless, the forms are not routinely used. *Child Protection: Messages from Research* was distributed by the Department of Health to 20,000 professionals in England and Wales. About 9,000 attended seminars and training events when the exercises included in the book, which were designed to show social workers that

the results of research are 'true for us' were used. Yet many professionals still say they have not heard of the 'blue book' and, judging from the questions of some researchers and policy makers asked at dissemination events, many of the messages were misunderstood.

Participants' rating of the *Going Home* materials compared with their involvement. The green lines shows the response from those who completed a booklet, the red line from those who had not.

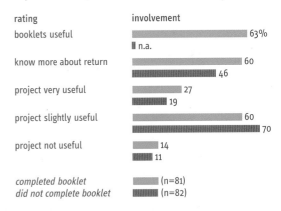

| rating | involvement | |
|---|---|---|
| booklets useful | | 63% |
| | n.a. | |
| know more about return | | 60 |
| | | 46 |
| project very useful | | 27 |
| | | 19 |
| project slightly useful | | 60 |
| | | 70 |
| project not useful | | 14 |
| | | 11 |
| *completed booklet* | (n=81) | |
| *did not complete booklet* | (n=82) | |

Thus, half the practitioners surveyed for the *Going Home* study had not completed a booklet, usually because they had not been responsible for any of the children looked after in the study period. Although those who had not used the materials were generally less enthusiastic about the project, the difference was not statistically significant. So it was not necessary for professionals to have completed a booklet for them to feel that they had gained from taking part. Over half in the participating authorities said they knew more about return as a result of their participation.

★ ★ ★

If professionals benefit from development tools, does practice alter as a result? It is a very difficult question to answer–and no great surprise that few have attempted to unravel it. The use of aggregated outcome data as a proxy measure of social work effectiveness, for instance, can be misleading: if outcomes for child and family are better in one area (say where a development exercise has been used) than in another (where no instruments have been available) the difference might be explained by any one of a host of factors, including, at one extreme, the variable competence of the social workers and, at another, the general circumstances of a local population. One might say that outcomes will likely reflect incomes as much as inputs.

In **Packman** and **Hall**'s recent study of the use of voluntary accommodation, this difficulty was resolved by comparing the same locations before and after the introduction of the *Children Act*, 1989. The evaluation process extended across a decade and relied upon two major investigations; it was successful, but only because it was conducted on a scale that could be justified in relation to a major innovation, such as new legislation. To apply

Packman, J. and Hall, C.
*From Care to Accommodation: Support, Protection and Control in Child Care Services,*
Stationery Office, London, 1998

equivalent resources to a relatively minor project like *Going Home* would be unthinkable. And even if the resources had been available, it would still be impossible to guarantee that any effect observed was attributable to any specific inputs: people vary from time to time as well as from place to place.

One potential solution is to run two distinct but comparable experiments in parallel, one of the approaches tried in the case of *Going Home,* the results from which are described in Chapter Nine. First the patterns of separation and return observed in the nine local authorities and certain, necessarily tentative, interpretations of the findings are worth recording.

Overall, better outcomes occurred when the *Going Home* booklets were completed. This is not to suggest that outcomes were positive because the booklets were filled in (in any case some of the associations are statistically quite weak), but it will be seen from the following table that, overall, when

The use of development tools and children's experience of return

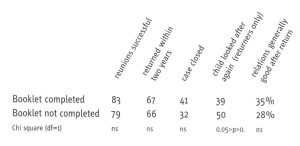

| | reunions successful | returned within two years | case closed | child looked after again (returners only) | relations generally good after return |
|---|---|---|---|---|---|
| Booklet completed | 83 | 67 | 41 | 39 | 35% |
| Booklet not completed | 79 | 66 | 32 | 50 | 28% |
| Chi square (df=1) | ns | ns | ns | 0.05>p>0. | ns |

the *Going Home* materials were applied, more children went home, were reunited successfully and did not need to be looked after again. It is even the case that family relations were better when the booklets were used, but the difference was statistically significant only among the considerably smaller proportion of children separated a second time (two-fifths of those for whom a booklet was completed; half of those for whom it was not).

These results were obtained by adding the totals for each local authority, so wide variations are disguised. For example, the proportion of separated children who went home within two years varied from 46% in one authority to 88% in another; authorities which used the booklets did not return a higher proportion of children looked after, nor were their returns any more or less successful. The development project was only one among a number of influences that appeared to affect patterns of separation and return within an authority.

Firstly, the *need* for out-of-home care was not constant between authorities. There is a complicated relationship between social and economic deprivation and patterns of separation and return in the child-care service. True, authorities coping with severe social and economic deprivation tend to look after a comparatively high proportion of their child population, particularly in the inner cities, but patterns in the rates for children starting to be looked after have been shown to be less distinct geographically than for children already looked after. So whereas London Borough had the lowest rate of admissions to care or accommodation and the second highest snapshot rate for children looked after, the comparatively affluent Southern Rural authority had the second highest rate of admission and the

second lowest rate for children looked after. Patterns of separation and return were undeniably influenced by socio-demographic factors but not necessarily in the expected direction.

The translation of patterns of need into services for children looked after varies from place to place. In a recent Dartington study concerning voluntary accommodation, reference is made to 'sore thumb syndrome' to describe a condition in which thresholds for admission to care or accommodation are lower in localities where a certain need is comparatively rare than where the same need is commonplace. The problems that afflict children and families tend to be less intractable in more affluent areas, and so the low level of deprivation is more likely to depress the number of separated children able to return home than the number in need of a brief separation. This tendency was certainly identifiable among the *Going Home* authorities and it can explain some of the variations just described.

Poverty is certainly one socio-demographic factor that has a bearing on decision making, but there are others. Social isolation, for example, which diminishes the network of friends and relatives to which parents can turn in time of crisis or for ordinary everyday support, is just as important, as authorities responsible for mobile populations, for example for a high proportion of first generation immigrants, well know. This was the case in London Borough, a third of whose looked after population had been born outside the UK. By comparison with other authorities, London Borough looked after children for relatively long periods.

Local authority policies will also have an impact on patterns of separation and return. For example, social services departments that give prominence to child protection services tend to look after comparatively large numbers of children away from home. The same is true of authorities that invest in respite care services. The amount an authority spends on vulnerable children will also have an effect. Within the authorities studied for *Going Home* however, the influence of such factors turned out to be negligible.

The results were a reminder of the conclusions to *Who Needs Care?* in which Packman and colleagues failed to identify any obvious relationship between the explicit aims of social services departments and patterns of substitute care. An authority with strong policies for keeping children out of care or accommodation is also less likely to return those it separates. Thus a policy will have unintended effects: more important, Packman says, are those assumptions and perspectives that guide everyday decision making within a social services department—what is conventionally called its ethos or culture.

With this research premiss in mind, a survey of professional attitudes towards child-care in the participating authorities was mounted part-way through the testing period. Reported in more detail in Chapter Eight, it confirms the connection Packman suggests: where children looked after were younger, professionals tended to adopt what Fox-Harding would call a child-protection perspective; where the equivalent population included more adolescents, the focus moved more in the direction of children's rights. Whether

practice creates perspective or vice versa is too complex a question to be discussed here, but it is clear that the professional view mediates between a research message conveyed by a development exercise and social worker response.

The conclusion must be that use of a developmental exercise, as measured by completion of the *Going Home* booklets, is associated with positive outcomes for children and families, as measured in this instance by patterns of separation and return. However, the association is conceivably attributable to a number of other factors, not least the socio-demography of local authorities and the ethos which prevails among the professional community. These issues are considered again in later chapters with the help of additional data, but first, to take rather a different tack, it is possible to deal with another question, 'Do the *Going Home* development tools have a more marked effect on the lives of children in particular circumstances?' Help with the answer is needed from another development exercise mentioned earlier, *Matching Needs and Services*.

*Matching Needs and Services* provides a mechanism for understanding patterns of need among different groups of children referred to children's services: those looked after, those requiring protection and family support, and those known to education, social services or health agencies.

The primary function of the *Matching Needs and Services* approach is to generate groupings of children in need that reflect local conditions and are meaningful to professionals, researchers and consumers. One hastens to add that the procedure

Packman, J. with Randall, J. and Jacques, N. *Who Needs Care? Social work decisions about children*, Basil Blackwell, Oxford, 1986

Fox Harding, L. *Perspectives in Child Care Policy*, Longman, London 1991

The impact of the *Going Home* materials on outcomes for children in different need groups

| Need group (at the point of separation) | % total sample (n=463) | % returning home in 'experimental' group (ie booklet used) | % returning home in control group (ie booklet not used) | Chi square (df=1) |
| --- | --- | --- | --- | --- |
| Multiple need, young children | 13 | 100 | 83 | ns |
| Chronic parenting problems | 10 | 100 | 90 | p<0.05 |
| Lone parents, several children | 20 | 89 | 78 | p<0.1 |
| Victims of severe abuse | 7 | 69 | 58 | ns |
| Voluntary accommodation reveals problems | 6 | 30 | 90 | p<0.05 |
| Adolescents with psychological problems | 4 | 100 | 86 | ns |
| Child behaviour and parenting problem | 6 | 61 | 90 | p<0.05 |
| Adolescents long neglected | 7 | 88 | 70 | p<0.1 |
| Family row | 22 | 94 | 98 | ns |
| Permanent alternative to home | 5 | 80 | 66 | ns |

has weaknesses and as this book goes to press has still to be fully validated. It is not yet possible to be confident, for instance, that someone using the method in Halifax with 100 children will come up with the same groupings as someone in Huddersfield making an assessment of the same cases, but the signs are reasonably good, and the method is certainly as useful as any other available for categorising groups of children looked after.

In the first *Matching Needs and Services* publication, ten groups are described which emerged from the pilot work and, with some variation, were subsequently found to apply in other test authorities. Differences were noted, for example, in departments coping with a large refugee population and where there were simply differences in nomenclature, so that there might be several ways of describing children in lone parent families but the needs remained very similar.

Each of the children in the *Going Home* evaluation was classified into one of the ten *Matching Needs and Services* groups. The allocation of cases was made by three researchers independently. In the 21% of cases where there was some disagreement as to which group a child belonged, case files were examined and the social worker was spoken to in order to find the best compromise. Return outcomes for the children were then evaluated and a comparison made between cases where the checklist booklets were or were not completed. The outcome measure chosen was the proportion of children returning within two years of separation, although similar results emerged for other indicators.

The results suggest that the materials made a difference to outcomes in relation to five of the ten need groups, but it is not possible to say whether the change was for the better or worse. There is an indication that use of the materials leads to more children returning when the primary need arises as a consequence of parenting difficulty; but where a period of voluntary accommodation uncovers new problems at home or there is some interaction between a child's misbehaviour and a parent's inability to control, use of the booklets reduces the proportion reunited with relatives–possibly a good thing.

In relation to the other need groups no significant effect was observed. Where the difficulty concerned serious abuse of a child, a breakdown in parent to parent (as opposed to parent to child) relationships, there was little benefit, similarly where a permanent alternative to the natural family was needed. Generally speaking, the materials are probably helpful in cases where relationships between parents and children have deteriorated but the parent does not want to lose the child (or the child his or her parent). The contribution they can make is much slighter when there are deep seated doubts about whether the child should be returned, conversely when it is universally accepted that return is the right course or where adolescents with psychological problems are concerned.

The moral for future development work must be that expectations of success or failure cannot be on a universal scale. To the blunt question, are the *Going Home* materials a good or a bad thing for professionals, children and families? one has to say, good for some, no benefit for some, not bad for many, and the same cautious response is likely to hold true for many other exercises like it. As researchers inch their way towards a taxonomy of children in need they will want managers and practitioners to increase the degree of differentiation in the services they offer, but there is also a similar message for researchers: in their development work they, too, must learn to differentiate between groups and to identify those that can benefit most from the application of research.

The *Going Home* project illustrates some of the difficulties to be encountered in getting research into practice and assessing the consequences. However available and accessible it is made, research information will not necessarily be consulted and where materials are used they will not necessarily make any difference to professional decision making. There is no reason why they

should: most children in the local authorities described here would have returned home quickly and successfully irrespective of any research input. Even in marginal cases, where the careful use of research knowledge might make a difference to client outcomes, there can be no guarantee that the effect will be sufficiently consistent to be visible in aggregate scores.

Moreover, there are many other telling sources of variation in the lives of children looked after and in local authorities: isolating the effects of a single variable, such as the application of a checklist on client outcomes is highly problematic. Even where there appears to have been an impact of some kind, it is not always easy to decide if it has been a positive one.

On the other hand, there are clearly cost benefits from applying a project like *Going Home*. A handful of more positive outcomes cannot be discounted, particularly considering that the additional input for each child was not an elaborate or expensive intervention involving long-term specialist foster care or residential placement but printed paper costing less than a pound and ten minutes of professional time. *Going Home* clearly did not make any major difference to patterns of separation and return in the authorities in which it was piloted, but it did improve the knowledge base of professionals. It was generally regarded as a useful supplement to professional decision making and it improved outcomes for five out of ten identified need groups.

# 8  Where do social workers get their information?

What do social workers read and whose advice do they want to hear? This chapter reports the answers practitioners themselves have given to these deceptively straightforward questions and goes on to discuss the implications for the organisers of research dissemination programmes.

Kuhn, T. *The Structure of Scientific Revolutions*, University of Chicago Press, 1962

Packman, J. *The Child's Generation: Child care policy in Britain*, Blackwell, 1981

The ideal would be to inject an idea or an important research finding with a dye and observe its progress through the social work profession's arterial system. In the days when the circulation of knowledge was achieved simply by the copying of manuscripts, the dissemination process was probably as easy to map; it was almost as visible. Even very recently, a shift in social work thinking such as that brought about by the movement around the *Children Act,* 1948 was comparatively easy to monitor. Packman (1981), for example, paints a vivid picture of the coherence achieved between research, policy development, training and practice in those days. The first group of student boarding-out officers at the London School of Economics was able to attend the debates on the *Children's Bill* in the Lords and witness the shaping of the legislation that they were to implement. These pioneers, Packman says, were then dispersed around the newly created children's departments, where their influence was 'far greater than their numbers would imply'.

Rarely has it been possible so unambiguously to follow the course of ideas and theories of practice between the spring of research and debate and the ocean of practice. As in other disciplines, most changes within the knowledge base of social work are incremental rather than revolutionary–they are what Kuhn called 'ordinary science' as opposed to 'paradigm shifts'. Little is known about how ideas and information percolate and come to influence the behaviour of individuals, professions or societies in the long gaps between major legislative upheavals.

Social work is considered distinctive because so little of its knowledge base is articulated, documented or codified. This is not to say that tacit understanding is unimportant–modern management literature lays great store by the wisdom accumulated through ordinary human relations–but it is consequently difficult to establish what social workers know and what they ought to know, let alone how best to communicate essential information to them.

Even when the work of a professional group is given coherence by overarching theories, there are obvious problems. The Advisory Group set up to examine the implementation of research findings in the NHS made the point:

considerable efforts are made to evaluate the

efficacy of different techniques for disseminating information to doctors and other care professionals. Relatively little work… has been devoted to the rigorous survey of where information currently used is drawn from. There is a considerable literature on innovation diffusion, the basis of clinical decision-making and the evaluation of specific ways of influencing physician behaviour… but little background work on current influences.

When the Advisory Group came to list research priorities within the NHS, to identify the main sources of information on health care effectiveness used by clinicians was put at number two. It is no less a priority within the personal social services. Since the pioneering studies by Wilson and colleagues at the University of Sheffield in the 1970s, very little work has been done in this area. What do social workers read and to whom do they listen? What difference does it make to their practice?

This chapter sets out the answers professionals themselves have given to these questions. The professional view is prone to the same weaknesses as any other process of self-report, but it nevertheless provides an indispensable starting point. If dissemination exercises like *Looking After Children*, *Going Home* and *Matching Needs and Services* are to have any lasting impact, the larger system in which they circulate needs to be understood.

With this in view, a survey was made of social workers with responsibility for children in need in six of the local authorities that took part in the *Going Home* study. In all, 163 social workers in 27 area teams were involved. All who were qualified at

degree level and who attended an ordinary team meeting completed the questionnaire. Such professionals with direct case responsibility represent only about 10% of all those employed by local authority social services departments but they have greatest responsibility for most day-to-day decisions regarding services for individual children and families. A check against data collected by the National Institute for Social Work (1993) confirmed that the age and gender balance of respondents was broadly in line with the national situation, so the survey could be considered to represent the views of a cross-section of the profession.

The survey dealt with three questions: first, what media are considered by the profession to be its main sources of information and ideas; second, how much variation is there within the broad patterns identified; third, is there any discernible difference in approach between those who claim to read research and those who disregard it. From the response it has been possible to develop a potential model for the dissemination of ideas and information in social work.

Social work professionals talk a lot. Conversation is the primary means for exchanging information. Over half (56%) of professionals frequently discuss cases with colleagues and view the exchanges as a good way of gaining knowledge. The status of the participants does not seem to be important, borne out by the finding that only a third (45%) of social workers frequently turn to their supervisor as a valuable source of information and a quarter never use supervision as a means of improving their understanding.

Wilson, T., Streatfield, D., Mullings, C., Smith, V. and Pendleton, B. *Information needs and information services in local authority social services departments*; final report to the British Library Research and Development Department (2vols.), University of Sheffield, 1978

As far as paper sources are concerned, the shorter and least obviously informed by research the piece, the more it will be read by social workers. *Community Care* is regularly read by nearly half (47%) of professionals but only a fifth (19%) frequently turn to specialist books and fewer still (15%) use national guidelines often. The most depressing finding was that 29% never read a specialist book and a fifth are willing to say they never open the guidance which effectively brings to life the *Children Act*, 1989. These revelations are summarised in the following graph.

Practitioners working directly with families were asked if they received information about current practice and research in relation to each item on the list 'often', 'sometimes' or 'never' and scored 2, 1 and 0 respectively. The mean shown here represents an aggregation of their responses.

'What emerged from the interviews with social workers was the importance of the Orange Book (*Protecting Childen: A guide for social workers undertaking a comprehensive assessment*, HMSO, 1988) as a source of ideas for assessment. Really nothing else seems to have taken root with practitioners in the same way. *Working Together* is likely to have been customised in the departmental procedures and appears not to have been much consulted by practitioners in the field, while the guidance on *Working with Child Sexual Abuse* (1991) was not mentioned by anybody.' From Fisher, T. *A Systematic Knowledge Base in Child Protection: What knowledge do social workers use?* Department of Social Policy and Social Work, University of York, 1995

Frequency with which social workers use different sources of information about current practice and research (the length of the line represents the mean score)

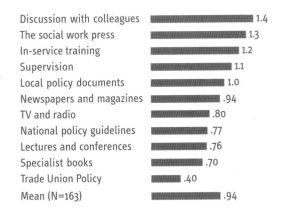

| Discussion with colleagues | 1.4 |
| The social work press | 1.3 |
| In-service training | 1.2 |
| Supervision | 1.1 |
| Local policy documents | 1.0 |
| Newspapers and magazines | .94 |
| TV and radio | .80 |
| National policy guidelines | .77 |
| Lectures and conferences | .76 |
| Specialist books | .70 |
| Trade Union Policy | .40 |
| Mean (N=163) | .94 |

The findings illustrate the gulf that still exists between research and practice, and the scale of the task facing agencies with disseminative roles. Researchers naturally feel most at home with forms of reporting over which they are most able to exercise a high degree of control. They are also professionally obliged to favour media that score highest in the reward systems of academic science–scholarly journals, academic books, policy guidelines, lectures and conferences. But these are precisely the media practitioners are least likely to acknowledge or to turn to for guidance.

An inevitable consequence is that the dissemination of ideas and information within social work commonly takes place within rather than between local authorities. Only the social work press has the distinction of being regularly used by social workers and having a circulation area broader than an individual authority.

Social work's preference for informal channels of communication has long been recognised, and much bemoaned. On this evidence, there is little to be gained from publishing more books or organising more conferences. It cannot be a question of accessibility when only 14% of social workers say they regularly use even the most prevalent media–television and radio–as a source of information. Similarly, national policy guidelines are published in huge quantities and given the widest possible circulation, but this does not guarantee that they are widely read. It emerged from Dartington's 1998 study, *Making Residential Care Work* that Volume Four of the *Children Act* Guidance was properly used in just three of the nine homes studied, a failing which considerably reduced the quality of care. Fisher's finding that most child protection guidance gathers dust on shelves, provides as little comfort.

A more encouraging view of the dissemination process can be gained from an alternative analysis of the data. It is possible to calculate a score for

In the tables on this and the facing page the mean is based on an aggregation of scores for 'low', 'medium' and 'high' familiarity with research. The accuracy of social workers' understanding of key findings in the literature on separation and return was also tested, if to a rather limited extent, *see page 85.*

individual respondents as well as for particular media, which will uncover a social worker's familiarity with research and can be used to distinguish between those who claim to receive research information from a variety of media and those who say they are less impressible. High scores will indicate a greater familiarity with research, or at least the claim to familiarity, than low scores. Separate respondents between low, middle or high scoring groups and it becomes possible to understand why some professionals use research and others do not.

Factors distinguishing levels of familiarity with research can be divided into individual factors, varying *within* locations, and environmental factors, varying *between* locations. The most important individual factors were a respondent's age and experience, and, not surprisingly, there was high correlation between the two. The next table shows that respondents in their twenties acknowledged a fairly limited exposure to research, but those in their fifties claimed greater awareness. This helps to explain a consistent finding in recent research that experienced social workers achieve better outcomes for children and families than the less experienced. However the picture is complicated by differences between generations. For example, younger social workers turn more readily to discussion and are increasingly reliant on supervision as a key information source—a welcome trend. Only one in six who qualified in the last five years considered the information they received during supervision to be unhelpful, compared with one in three among those who qualified in the 1970s.

Research familiarity by age of respondent (the length of the line represents the mean score)

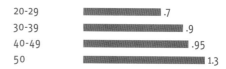

| | |
|---|---|
| 20-29 | .7 |
| 30-39 | .9 |
| 40-49 | .95 |
| 50 | 1.3 |

It is less encouraging to discover that half of the recently qualified said they did not obtain information from lectures and conferences, compared with a quarter of those who had qualified in the 1970s. Worse still, fewer than one in ten of the less-experienced said they used national policy guidelines often. These findings hold true regardless of length of service, so that a 29-year-old social worker with eight years' experience is as unlikely to use Department of Health guidance as a 22-year-old settling into his first post. Although such an interpretation is not to be drawn from the data described here, it seems that these generation trends reflect changes in the general training of social workers.

Several factors might account for the findings. First, there is the question of access to the various sources of information—for example, certain local authorities may deliberately restrict attendance on training courses to more senior personnel. However, *Access Disputes in Child Care,* which studied the workings of the *HASSASSA Act 1983,* indicated that there were informal procedures at work: even when the Codes of Practice that accompanied the Act reached district offices, they were seldom distributed among all professional colleagues. A second reason concerns organisational responsibilities: those in senior positions are expected to give rather than take advice, whether formally in supervision or informally over coffee.

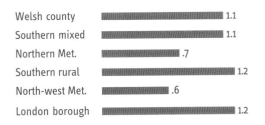

Research familiarity in the six local authorities where the questionnaire was used (the length of the line represents the mean score).

Welsh county — 1.1
Southern mixed — 1.1
Northern Met. — .7
Southern rural — 1.2
North-west Met. — .6
London borough — 1.2

Differences between authorities are more likely to be explained by environmental factors. Social workers in the two Northern metropolitan boroughs had the least familiarity with research: well over half never turned to evidence of the kind produced by research units and a higher proportion still said they had never opened the *Children Act* guidance. The picture was rather better in Welsh County and Southern-mixed and the best results were returned in Southern rural and London Borough (where, incidentally, the *Going Home* materials were most avidly consumed).

Familiarity with research seemed to reflect the prevailing organisational climate. It was not that one structural arrangement was better than another, rather that stability was preferable to change. Professionals are understandably more receptive to research when their team is stable, morale is high, there is a shared outlook and

resources are reasonably good. Such conditions were as influential within authorities as between them. An interesting chicken and egg question, not to be tackled here, is whether high morale and a shared outlook encourage or reflect a keener interest in research and policy.

Experienced social workers operating in stable teams that give research and guidance their worth are the most likely to use evidence when making decisions. It is noteworthy that social workers who read research tend to read everything: guidance, newspapers and even local authority and trade union policy papers. However, there is also at least one contra-indication to report; both the Northern Met. authorities, which employed professionals who least used research, made good use of the *Going Home* materials. Among those otherwise starved of research knowledge, the materials seemed to provide an interesting if isolated diversion.

In the closing chapters, more complex designs are used to evaluate the impact of research. Here, the issue is the extent to which professionals themselves consider that such information affects them. In the main, social workers are aware that their practice is affected by the information they absorb. But there are anomalies: specialist books (but not *Children Act* guidance) have a greater than expected influence on practice, given that they are read so infrequently; news media, including newspapers, TV, radio and the social work press are perceived by social workers as having a smaller impact upon their actions than might be expected, given their considerable exposure to it. The principal influence upon practice is considered to be in-service training–paradoxically an avenue seldom explored by researchers.

Professionals' perception of which media most affect their practice (the length of the line represents the mean score)

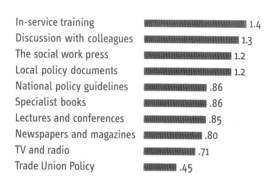

| | |
|---|---|
| In-service training | 1.4 |
| Discussion with colleagues | 1.3 |
| The social work press | 1.2 |
| Local policy documents | 1.2 |
| National policy guidelines | .86 |
| Specialist books | .86 |
| Lectures and conferences | .85 |
| Newspapers and magazines | .80 |
| TV and radio | .71 |
| Trade Union Policy | .45 |

The same social workers were asked to indicate if the following statements were true in all, some or hardly any of their cases

- Twelve year olds know what is in their own best interests.
- Parents are children's most important source of support.
- Social workers do as much harm as good.
- Partnership with families results in the best possible outcome for a child.
- Parents are the source of most children's problems.
- Admission to care or accommodation benefits parents more than children.
- The only 'solution' to sexual abuse is to remove the perpetrator.

Another mechanism used to measure the difference research made to social work was to ask the practitioners to indicate the extent to which they agreed or disagreed with several practice statements. Their replies were compared with what they said about their use of information to discover if there was any relationship between a familiarity with research and individual opinion. The list of statements appears at the side of the page. High users of research were more likely than low scorers to agree with the statement 'partnership with families results in the best possible outcome for a child' and to disagree with the statement that 'admission to care or accommodation benefits parents more than children'. Although these correlations were on the margins of statistical significance, they suggest some association between a professed avowed openness to research findings and a particular form of practice wisdom. However, the processes by which research information feeds into individual practice decisions are too obscure to attempt to analyse by means of a self-report questionnaire. The same issues are addressed with a more appropriate methodology in the next chapter.

A survey of child-care practitioners may not be the ideal way to discover what social workers know, where they get their information from or how they use it, but it does serve to illustrate the complexities of research dissemination. Most information is passed on by word of mouth, sometimes formally through structures such as supervision and in-service training, but usually informally through discussion. The core content of this conversation is likely to be published material, so although research reports and policy guidelines may not be widely read, whatever is read is likely to be widely disseminated. Supervision in social work provides a unique structure for the dissemination of ideas and information, one that other professions might envy. And there is an indication in the survey data that younger social workers regard supervision as a valuable source of information.

How, then, when they are so rarely read, do research reports provide the germ of the practice wisdom of a senior practitioner? How are researchers to bridge the gap between the written and the spoken word, and between central and local government? The diagram on the facing page indicates the pathways of research dissemination within social work, based on this survey. The

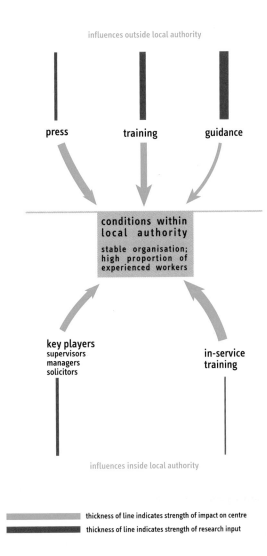

influences outside local authority

press      training      guidance

**conditions within local authority**

**stable organisation; high proportion of experienced workers**

**key players**
supervisors
managers
solicitors

**in-service training**

influences inside local authority

thickness of line indicates strength of impact on centre
thickness of line indicates strength of research input

central box represents a local authority. The ideal conditions for research usage in any social services department have been found to be a stable organisation which supports an experienced staff group, a high proportion of whom are willing to learn. The influences on the authority are shown as green arrows of varying strength; some (indicated below the box) operating inside the social services department; others, including the press, training and guidance, outside. Thus the social work press has been found to be consulted far more frequently than the *Children Act* guidance.

The secondary band of red arrows indicates the impact research evidence makes on these influences. They also are of varying strength so that while there are close links between research and guidance, there has tended to be little reference to evidence in the social work press.

The majority of Dartington's scientific development work and dissemination activity has been aimed directly at the professional – *Going Home, Looking After Children* and *Structure and Culture in Residential Care* are examples. In future, certain other avenues may turn out to be more profitable and perhaps most important: in-service training and supervision, which act as a channel between research and policy at the national level and within local practice. Social work trainers are expected to be up-to-date; they are usually based inside local authorities but rely on ideas and information in circulation outside. They are mediators and ideally placed to act as a link between research and practice.

The survey demonstrates that research dissemination is much more a 'process' than an 'event'. Thus, social workers obtain their information from the figure immediately above them in an informal information hierarchy: for a novice social worker, this will probably be a senior colleague, for a team leader it will probably be a trainer, for a trainer, it is less likely to be a person than a book or lecture transcript. These conclusions mirror those reached by Wilson and colleagues in their far more extensive studies. They are also the equivalent of the kind of ripple effect on which management gurus base their formulae for effective change, though at times the ripples will be difficult to discern and in some local authorities the water is fairly stagnant.

What are the implications of such findings for cost-effective research development and dissemination? Firstly, if there is a short-cut to research dissemination it undoubtedly lies in the direction of the social work press. It is relied upon by front-line professionals as a source of research and practice information in a way that other published and broadcast materials clearly are not. And in their references to the social work press, practitioners mean news magazines like *Community Care* rather than any academic journal. How *Community Care* compares to other trade papers such as *The Nursing Times* or the *British Medical Journal*, in the presentation of research is for others to judge, but the recent introduction of *Research Matters*, a joint effort between the ADSS and *Community Care*, would seem to bode well for the future.

Secondly, the survey emphasises the importance of targeting what advertisers refer to as opinion-formers—senior staff with responsibility for training and/or supervision in regular face-to-face contact with caseworkers, rather than the caseworkers themselves. Finally, more thought could be given by researchers to the means by which such trainers can best help professionals convert research findings into messages about good practice in specific agencies at specific times. The Department of Health's summaries of research, for example, each contained a series of 'True for Us?' exercises, which appear to have been very successful.

Lord Northbrook famously bemoaned the fact that while he knew that half the money he spent on advertising was wasted, he could not say which half. A newspaper tycoon might get away with such a confession of ignorance, but those who accept responsibility for a programme of public sector research development and dissemination in the 1990s must aim higher.

The practitioner response to our survey re-emphasises the central role to be played in research dissemination by those media and personnel with one foot in the camp of practice and the other in that of research and policy. It seems sensible to conclude that these interdisciplinary channels are the most likely to reward the investment of resources.

# 9 Experiments to test ultimate outcomes

*This chapter describes the two most detailed and extensive tests made of the effectiveness of the Going Home development materials and explains how the results have been used in planning new approaches to the problems of translating research knowledge into sound evidence-based practice*

## 1 In a Southern Rural county

It is fairly easy to calculate the costs of applying research. Research and development costs represent the greatest investment, but, over time, in the case of a project like *Going Home,* the investment is at the level of about two pounds for every child the materials are used to help. Implementation may add another three pounds to the bill per child, most of that additional spending being attributable to the professional time taken to complete the form–but the costs are very modest when compared to the several hundred thousand pounds, depending on the length of stay and placement, required to support a typical case. Whether or not *Going Home* represents a good investment for a local authority, it can hardly be considered a major risk, at least in financial terms.

By any standards, *Going Home* represented a minor modification of social work practice. But could it reap benefits that might justify even a marginal place in a social worker's repertoire? The results in terms of immediate and intermediate outcomes were promising; the real test, however, concerned the ultimate outcome. To measure this aspect of the project's effectiveness, two

experiments were made, both making a comparison between an area where the materials were used and another where no additional equivalent support was offered. Both tests used resources in addition to the materials: in Southern Rural a Professor of Social Work collaborated with practitioners; in Midlands County, the subject of the second part of this chapter, the emphasis was on training and support.

In Southern Rural the lion's share of resources was invested in two children and families' social work teams where use of the checklists, books and guides was supplemented by monthly visits from an experienced trainer and researcher from Bristol University, Professor Phyllida Parsloe. Professor Parsloe was commissioned by the Research Unit to help social workers to get the most out of the materials; outcomes for children in the two teams were then compared with those in neighbouring locations. Professor Parsloe worked in the experiment area; the results she obtained were compared with those from the control area where there was no access to the *Going Home* materials.

In the experiment area, which comprised a

---

Ease of use has to be a common aspiration among research developers. Anything a researcher (or a developer for that matter) asks of a practitioner is bound to be regarded as additional work. The idea must be that extra effort at one stage in the process will save time later on. Five minutes considering questions about reunion at the point of separation might speed a reunion and make it more successful. Two hours filling in *Looking After Children* forms with a child appears time consuming, but set against the 2,500 hours spent sheltering a typical long-stay case, two hours is next to nothing. The *Matching Needs and Services* approach requires the help of several people for a week, sometimes longer, but the reward is a better planned range of local authority services and more skilful use of several million pounds from the public purse.

Phyllida Parsloe is known mainly for her work on juvenile delinquency but in the 1970s also researched the ways social workers practised. The experiment could never, of course, be replicated. Professors of Social Work are expensive resources and it would be impracticable to introduce one in all social work teams. But it was hoped to learn something about how practitioners might be encouraged to use research in the context of a busy schedule.

division of the county, one team was located in the second largest town, the other in a seaside resort. Both covered fairly extensive country areas as well as an urban base. The programme Professor Parsloe agreed with the practitioners included monthly meetings with each team, each lasting 90 minutes. The plan was that as many staff as possible should attend each meeting but it was acknowledged that attendances were likely to fluctuate. Like the experiment area, the comparison location comprised two medium-sized towns surrounded by agricultural districts. Experiment and comparison areas looked very similar by most socio-demographic indicators and since they both came under the same Assistant Director there was little, if any, variation in policy or organisation.

Professor Parsloe's view was that the meetings would increase the use of the checklists, provide a commentary on the research so encouraging its use, and therefore, achieve the best ultimate outcomes, an improved experience for children and families. This intention largely mirrored the researchers' objectives that the programme would encourage both more frequent and more sophisticated use of the research materials, which would ultimately be reflected in improved outcomes for children looked after and their families. The actual effects of the process were evaluated at the immediate, intermediate and ultimate levels described above.

*Going Home* booklets were begun for just over half (53%) the children and young people separated from their families in the experiment area. Nationally, booklets were commenced for exactly half (50%). As the diagram on the facing page

shows, among the nine authorities three scored lower than Southern Rural or achieved a similar result and three did rather better. Against this criterion then, there was no significant improvement in the experiment area. Even where booklets were started, they were seldom filled in at the time of separation. Those begun were rarely completed beyond the period of Professor Parsloe's direct involvement. Since the booklets were specifically designed to be used throughout the period of a child's separation, the findings were disappointing and frustrating.

Why did the extra input seem to make so little difference? Those involved blamed pressure of work: staff explained that there was a great deal of paperwork to complete when a child was separated from home and that forms that secured resources–for example a foster bed–always took priority. There was a perception that, far from being a useful tool, the checklists merely added a new dimension to the chronic bureaucratic overload. It was discovered that professionals made a distinction between completion and use where form-filling was concerned: one in the Southern Rural experiment area noted that 'if the forms were required by the local authority or the Department of Health they would be filled in, but not used'. (It was just this kind of impasse–how to ensure that materials were used to best advantage without making them compulsory–that the experiment with Professor Parsloe had been designed to address.) Others disliked the checklist booklet for the clinical approach it represented and on the grounds that it failed to capture the perspectives of child and family. A practitioner even suggested that two different checklists might be a better plan, one for service providers, another for users, even as the researchers were mulling over the signal inability among his colleagues to complete just one.

Completion rates for the local authorities

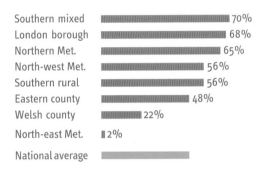

| | |
|---|---|
| Southern mixed | 70% |
| London borough | 68% |
| Northern Met. | 65% |
| North-west Met. | 56% |
| Southern rural | 56% |
| Eastern county | 48% |
| Welsh county | 22% |
| North-east Met. | 2% |
| National average | |

It was important to try to establish whether professionals felt that their decision making was affected by participation in the project and the insight into research findings it gave them. Unless there was evidence that professionals made decisions different from those they might otherwise have taken, there could be no point in asking whether those decisions were better or worse.

Here too, the results were once more disappointingly equivocal and in some cases downright dispiriting: for example, apparently none of the staff had regarded the *Going Home* booklets as a predictive tool, nor did they check their judgements about return against the checklists. Lack of familiarity with the use of research in planning and decision making was also evident: for example, confusion about precisely

when one of the checklists should be completed was resolved by a decision to complete it *after* the first major planning meeting which took place with the family and the child, when the stated intention was that the tools should contribute to the discussion and inform the plan. Similarly, for some children long looked after, social workers assumed that the booklet was to be filled in after the child had returned home. Any potential the materials had for improving decision making was unlikely to exploited if they were only to be consulted after the important planning decisions had been made.

More worrying than neglect was the evidence of abuse: some participants appeared to interpret the *Going Home* project as having the aim of getting children home at all costs. Even those who read the research with Professor Parsloe came to that opinion when the central thrust of the research was quite clearly not that most children necessarily *should* go home but that most *do*–that perhaps some who do should not and, in any case, that there are many technical interventions professionals can make to improve outcomes. The discovery that the findings could be so seriously misinterpreted, that children might go home unnecessarily or more quickly than was right or safe had a nightmarish quality. To learn that the project was consequently being considered at best pointless and at worst potentially dangerous in an area where it was supposedly being painstakingly tested was hardly a moment of discovery to savour.

Thankfully, the doubts, confusion and misinterpretation apparent at the time Professor Parsloe was actually visiting the Southern Rural team gave way to a more positive ethos when practitioners came to reflect on the usefulness of her work. Asked 18 months later, *all* the professionals said they found the materials useful, *all* said they found the exercise useful or at worst slightly useful and three-fifths felt they knew more about risks and remedies in the area of separation and return. These later results were better than those found in the other participating authorities.

Eighteen months later, then, professionals seemed to have developed some belated regard for the project but still it appeared to be the indirect benefits that were most appreciated, rather than the intended direct benefits of applying the research materials. Particularly important among the gains was the time for reflection created by the meetings. Participants also spoke warmly of Professor Parsloe's contributions. It was as much the self-confidence they gained from her support and encouragement as the perceptiveness of her analysis that they valued. It seems reasonable to conclude that participation in the project did have an effect on social work decision making, but it was because it created a safe space for discussion, not because it  permitted more wide-ranging or more sophisticated use of research findings. It is not realistic to seek to extend the chain of cause and effect from a general, unspecified effect on decision making to improved outcomes for children and families: research can help to maximise the probability of success, but it cannot guarantee it. Nevertheless, and for obvious reasons, the proof of the research development pudding is, for many people, in the outcome eating.

Some caution must be exercised when interpreting the following, quite promising results. The number of children involved in the Southern Rural experiment was small; 30 in the experiment area and 24 in the comparison group. As will be seen, far more cases were available in the Midland County experiment. It also turned out that the population of children being looked after in the Southern Rural experiment and control areas were slightly different. There were more boys in the comparison (63%) than in the experiment teams (50%) and it is known that boys are slower to return than girls. That said, in nearly all other respects, including age, race and previous care careers, the two groups were very similar.

Roughly the same proportion of children went home within 24 months in the experiment (77%) and comparison areas (79%). All estimates of outcome were made at a point two years after separation. Social workers' misapprehensions that research would propel children home when they should stay away seemed to have been appropriately dealt with.

But for half the children in the experiment area the case was kept open when they went home and social workers put the research messages into practice by supporting families through the difficult moments of reunion. This proportion was significantly greater than in the comparison area (17%) or the national survey (28%).

The consequence of increasing social work activity when children in the experimental area returned home was that far more reunions were successful. Outcomes were judged to be good if the reunion lasted for as long as the child (where he or she was old enough to express a judgement) the carer and the social worker considered it appropriate. In most cases this meant *ad infinitum* but for some adolescents an appropriate period could mean just a few weeks. Against this criterion, three-quarters (74%) of cases in the experiment area return were found to be successful against fewer than two-fifths (37%) in the comparison group.

The next link in the chain of beneficial effect is that far fewer children in the experiment area were looked after for a second period. Repeated sojourns in care or accommodation are not necessarily a bad thing, but the difference between the two groups was significant: repeat prescriptions were applied to just 13% of the experiment area children but to 95% of those in the comparison group. By most observers' standards the performance of the experimental group will be regarded as a considerable achievement.

Closer scrutiny shows that, in the experiment area, successful reunions were associated not only with keeping the social work files open but also with longer separations. In the comparison group half of those separated were home within ten days, but several months had elapsed before a comparable proportion was achieved by the experiment group. Thus, by taking a cautious approach to return, the teams advised by Professor Parsloe achieved more positive results. Far from jeopardising children's welfare by encouraging social workers to get children home at almost any costs, as feared, the project appeared to have achieved exactly the opposite, allowing professionals to step back from daily pressures and take a more balanced view of the issues.

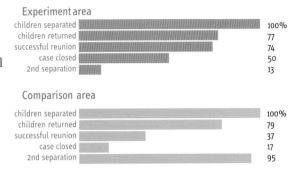

Return outcomes for children and families in the experiment and comparison location in Southern Rural

**Experiment area**

| | |
|---|---|
| children separated | 100% |
| children returned | 77 |
| successful reunion | 74 |
| case closed | 50 |
| 2nd separation | 13 |

**Comparison area**

| | |
|---|---|
| children separated | 100% |
| children returned | 79 |
| successful reunion | 37 |
| case closed | 17 |
| 2nd separation | 95 |

Separations were longer as a consequence, but reunions more enduring and the experience of children and families improved.

At the start of the Chapter, questions were raised about the impact of research development on social work practice and about the cost in the context of social services investment in needy children and families. By most reckoning, there was an 'ultimate' pay off in Southern Rural's experiment in the sense that social workers' decision making was influenced–largely for the better–by the research.

But there are costs to be weighed: the time spent discussing the research with Professor Parsloe; two extra months of foster, residential or some other kind of substitute care; continued social work support once the child was back at home–all these represent an increased financial burden for the local authority. On the other hand, they can be set against savings to be made in terms of placement costs; nearly all the comparison group children returned to local authority placements. The Dartington Unit does not have the expertise to calculate the cost-benefits precisely but it is inclined to the view that *Going Home* saved Southern Rural money or at least encouraged social workers to secure substantial benefits for children and families at no extra cost.

The experiment provided a reminder of what social workers can achieve: they can do little to influence the fact of return but they can change its timing, the manner in which it is accomplished and, therefore, its outcome. Between the experiment and comparison areas there was hardly any difference in the proportion of children who returned home within two years: indeed, the rate of about 80% mirrors that found nationally and is much the same today as it was a decade ago, but in the experimental area, professionals could modify the rate of return, work with families to overcome problems and reduce anxiety as the reunion progressed.

Taken on its own, the experiment suggests that attempts to focus the minds of professionals on issues of return and rehabilitation can pay dividends but that there are many ways to get good results. Paradoxically, the immediate effect of Professor Parsloe's involvement was to reduce participants' commitment to the research materials; ultimately, however, the effect that the research team was hoping for–better decision making–was achieved.

What are the lessons for those wishing to develop research messages for practice? First there is plainly benefit in activity supplementary to the use of development materials. Whether Professor Parsloe was the right person for the job is difficult to gauge, but the qualities she brought to the task, of objective scrutiny, a readiness to read the research and to apply it to real case examples, in addition to the accepted social work virtues of compassion and support, are those one would want to bring to bear. Second, there is almost always an initial resistance to research knowledge and the *Going Home* study and the development materials were no exception. Consequently, the research messages were misinterpreted and, for whatever reason, Professor Parsloe was unable to correct the mistake. But first impressions are not necessarily unalterable: in the case of Southern Rural, the effect of the encounter was to encourage social workers to reflect on decisions in the light of the findings and to be more considered in their actions. The result beyond small short-term costs brought children and families long-term benefits.

# Experiments to test ultimate outcomes
## 2 In a Midlands county

In Midlands County, one of the largest local authorities in the country, between 30 and 40 children begin a fresh episode of being looked after every month, with the result that over 1,000 are being looked after at any one time. This number is partly attributable to a considerable volume of respite care both with foster families and in two specialist residential centres. The rate of children looked after is about the same as that found nationally, 47 per 10,000, but the rate at which children are separated from parents is considerably lower than in England as a whole, suggesting a reluctance, prior to the experiment starting, to resort to substitute care. This pattern is confirmed by the findings that far fewer children were accommodated under voluntary arrangements–in other words, separations were generally ratified by a court–and that four-fifths of those looked after had been away from home for over a year.

The south and west of the county were heavily industrialised, there was a belt of agricultural land in the centre and to the north-east a rugged region largely dependent on tourism. The needs and problems of the county's inhabitants were likewise extremely varied, ranging from the isolation and limited resources typical of rural farming communities to problems of violent crime and drug abuse more often associated with inner-cities.

The experimental approach was quite different from the small-scale, resource-intensive exercise attempted in Southern Rural. Midlands County provided an opportunity to assess the potential effects of a research development project across a large, heterogeneous area, where the number of children looked after represented two per cent of the national total. The size and variety of the area made it rather difficult to identify representative experiment and comparison areas, as had been done in Southern Rural. It would clearly be misleading, for example, to attempt to compare a conurbation with a sparsely populated National Park; instead, the nine administrative districts were divided into two roughly comparable groups. Although none of the administrative districts could individually be considered the equivalent of any other, it was possible to pick two groups (five districts in one, four in the other) which were more or less equal in terms of their range of economic and demographic profiles.

The aim was to develop a cost-effective way of reaching large groups of social workers that might achieve benefits similar to those obtained from the concentrated involvement in Southern Rural. In the experimental area of Midlands County a study day was organised around the research materials; the comparison area, by contrast, was not directly informed that any such project was taking place. Wherever possible, it was the intention to prevent contamination between the two groups, for example by discouraging the transfer of materials and information between the two. As will be seen, keeping the two populations apart was easier said than done, but as a test of the *Going Home* materials it was the most robust experiment yet attempted. The outcomes evaluated were the same as those for Southern Rural; namely frequency of research use, better social work decisions and improved experiences for children and families.

Comparing outcomes between test areas was complicated by a wide variation in practice. For example, one team working in the experimental area was responsible for only four separations during the study period, so it could hardly be regarded as a triumph for research that booklets had been completed in each case. This was a comparatively affluent, rural district, where the fact that a child was to be looked after was rare enough to cause a *frisson* of excitement in the local office.

What may have been quite an elegant solution to the difficulties of ensuring comparability also created political difficulties. The lack of choice within county areas about whether to participate led to a degree of suspicion and resentment among some social workers, which was compounded by a coincidental freeze on recruitment following a budget overspend. Inevitably, the most overstretched teams felt the cuts hardest and one in the experimental half of the county became involved in a dispute with the treasurer. *Going Home* was never going to be high on the agenda of managers and social workers caught up in a political dispute. No booklets were completed during the study.

Personnel factors also came into play. One area manager, for example, took early retirement in the middle of the project. Her departure was part of a major restructuring that tended to blur the clear administrative divisions on which the experiment relied. A year into the study the distinction between experimental and comparison groups could still be made, but there had been a transformation of the organisational structure inside each. Despite considerable enthusiasm for

the project at the start, the priority it received gradually diminished.

In the experimental half of the County booklets were completed for just over a quarter (28%) of those separated, but the figure masks the variation just described. If the score obtained in the 'best' area had been repeated in the 'worst', booklets would have been completed for two thirds of the cohort. Discounting the area where there was the financial dispute and no booklets were completed at all, the completion rate was nearly half (48%), much the same as the national average and very close to what would have been predicted by the model advanced in Chapter Six..

The work in Midlands County was designed to discover whether decisions made in experiment and control locations were consistently different. In the first instance, professionals were asked if they felt better informed as a result of using the materials. On the day of their induction training they completed a questionnaire and 18 months later they were asked to do so again as part of a general feedback to all professionals, including those from the comparison locations who were asked to respond to the same questions for the first and only time.

The model generated a great deal of information, much of which has been used to inform the discussion in the earlier sections of the book. The intention here is to concentrate on a single aspect of the questionnaire that has a broad bearing on decision making concerning reunion: the accuracy of social workers' knowledge of the proportion of separated children who eventually return.

DATAR is trying to bring together under one roof practitioners, researchers, managers, children and families and so clear away the bureaucratic clutter that seems to accumulate between them when they operate from their own territory. For practitioners it has created an opportunity to do some small research of their own; perhaps as usefully, on the other side of the bargain, it has made it possible for qualified researchers to do some social work.

As the graph below shows, at the first time of asking, fewer than a fifth (17%) of practitioners in the experiment area gave the correct answer of 92%, even within a range of five per cent. Indeed, at the outset more social workers (26%) thought that less than a quarter of looked after children went home.

Such a finding was a graphic, depressing example of the gap between research knowledge and practice wisdom. It led to considerable reflection upon the role of organisations like the Dartington Unit and influenced the thinking that led to the creation of Research in Practice and a local 'teaching hospital' initiative called Dartington and Teignbridge Active Research and brought to the fore ideas about evidenced based social work described in the closing chapter.

From this low baseline, the first comparison could be made. Did social workers in the experiment area know better as a result of their exposure to the *Going Home* materials and their brief induction training? The answer was undoubtedly 'yes'. Only five per cent of those asked

at the end of the project thought that fewer than half looked after children eventually went home and nearly three-quarters (71%) got the answer more or less correct.

Encouraged by this finding, a second comparison was made, between the improved knowledge of those in the experimental area and that of their colleagues in Midland County. Here the results were not as expected, although the contamination that had occurred turned out to be much as the researchers had feared. During the 18 month period, practitioners in the comparison group talked to their colleagues in the experimental area and were affected by the same process of transmission described in earlier Chapters. This process was aggravated by the reorganisation that took place half-way through the experiment, as well as by the ordinary movement of staff from one part of the county to another. Services, like residential care, provided to both halves of the county were found to be an important conduit of information. This result was a blow to the methodologists in the research team, but extremely useful to those seeking to understand the dissemination of ideas.

The contamination of the comparison group made it necessary to re-evaluate the experiment. In effect, the work had created three groups of professionals; those (in the experimental group) who had received training and had gone on to use the *Going Home* materials, those (also in the experiment group) who had been trained in the use of the materials but never actually used them when working with a looked after child, and, third, those in the comparison group who had not been

Research in Practice was established in 1996 to give services for children and families managed by local authorities in England and Wales stronger links with the research community and to help them make better use of research findings. It tries to be distinctive by working with everyone involved in the planning and delivery of services to children and their families, identifying, sifting and sorting the most useful research information and delivering it in a variety of media, providing opportunities for planners and managers to work out ways to promote greater research mindedness within their agencies, and identifying opportunities for service agencies to have greater purchase on the national research agenda. One of the main ambitions of Research in Practice is thus to make it easier for local authorities to exchange useful information and to develop practical strategies for dealing with social care issues.

These results suggest that in the absence of good information, professionals may as well pick an answer out of a hat as rely upon their intuition. Does it matter that professionals estimate the chances not only so poorly, but with such little consistency? Common sense would answer 'yes'. An informed decision must be better than an uninformed decision, almost by definition.

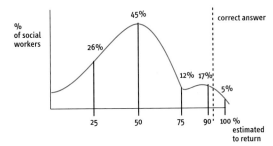

trained, were never asked to use the materials but, by their contact with colleagues in the experimental areas, had picked up the essential facts.

Now to take a second indication of professional decision making: the speed with which children were returned. Initially, it can be said that slightly more children in the experimental areas (74%) were home with relatives within six months of leaving than in the other locations (68%). But where social workers had completed the booklets, nearly all (95%) children were back within six months. The experimental social workers who never used the materials seemed to make roughly the same decisions as those who were never exposed to them.

A decision to send a child home quickly is not the same thing as a good outcome. To make that judgement the same test that had been used in Southern Rural was applied, namely whether a reunion lasted for as long as the child (where he or she was old enough to express a judgement), the carer and the social worker considered appropriate.

Again, completion of the *Going Home* material was found to make a difference. Nearly three-fifths (57%) of children whose social worker had been trained in and had used the *Going Home* materials experienced a successful reunion. Where the professionals did not use the booklets, outcomes were roughly the same as in the comparison areas–successful in about two-fifths of cases. The experiment in Midlands County tried to establish whether improvements in knowledge, decision making and outcomes for children and families might be achieved by applying simple research measures across a wide geographical area.

But local authorities are not laboratories, and so there is likely always to be a fundamental conflict between the need to bring scientific rigour to the pursuit of good data and to engage the consultative processes on which consensual change in a large organisation normally depends. The method in this case called for a random allocation of individuals, which inevitably conflicted with the fundamental social work principle that individuals should have a say in the decisions made on their behalf.

The original intention was to compare two contrasting practitioner groups, one fully committed to the project, the other entirely unaware of its existence. In the event there was a continuum of involvement in which the majority of professionals were neither fully committed nor entirely unaware. Maintaining the distance between them was made more difficult when the county was restructured in midstream.

In the end, the work in Midlands County contained too much science for the social workers and too much social work for the scientists. The results might be considered an example of a so-called Hawthorne effect: they are certainly a reminder that research is itself a dissemination process. The results require careful interpretation, but they are nevertheless encouraging: they demonstrate, for example, that the process of research dissemination continues long after the conference tables have been put away and researchers have moved on to new topics. They also provide evidence that good research development is associated with positive results for children and families.

Mention of 'Hawthorne effects' refers to a series of experiments at the Western Electric Company in Chicago between 1927 and 1932. Lighting levels were improved in one workshop but not in another in order to demonstrate that output and morale were raised by better working conditions. The unexpected result was that output in both workshops improved. The fact that humane attention was being given to workers' needs–in this case by the researchers themselves–was found to be the more vital factor.

There is another set of comparisons to be made between the experimental groups in Southern Rural, where the input was expensive and intensive, and Midlands County, where the contribution might be described as quick and dirty. The social workers Phyllida Parsloe assisted were slower to return their children than their equivalents in Midlands County who eagerly completed the booklets, and they also achieved better outcomes with a higher percentage of children (74% in Southern Rural compared to 57% in Midlands County).

The greater the input the better the outcome would seem to be the conclusion of this analysis. On the other hand, at the end of the project, three-quarters of the social workers in Midlands County were well-appraised of the fact that nearly all children return home, which, despite the very considerable dissemination efforts of the last 15 years, beginning with the publication of *Social Work Decisions in Child Care*, probably distinguishes them from their colleagues across the country.

Clearly, the chief obstacle to greater and more precise use of research in professional decisionmaking is not professional resistance but simply the low priority accorded to research on the professional agenda. Training, legislation, tradition and policy dictate a wide range of responsibilities to social workers without indicating how they should be prioritised. As long as tasks such as the use of the *Going Home* checklists continue to be regarded in the same tiresome bureaucratic bracket as record-keeping and administration they will continue to take a low priority. If they are ever seen as important enough to displace some other activity, they will have to be reclassified in the professional mind as an equivalent of casework.

Is this a plausible ambition? The decision by participants in Southern Rural to complete checklists after rather than before planning meetings signifies the role that research is seen to occupy in social work–as an irritating appendix to proper practice. Where there is goodwill, professionals will go through the motions. Where goodwill is in short supply, as in the impoverished quarter of Midlands County, they may refuse to participate altogether. There is a vicious circle in operation here–unless research findings are used to inform decision making, research will remain a burden on professionals who have better things to do. As long as research is seen as a burden rather than an opportunity, it is unlikely to be used to inform decision making.

To take a more optimistic view: the more research findings are formally integrated into practice on a daily basis, the more such findings can be formally generated almost as a by-product of practice. The *Looking After Children* materials provide the best current example of such a structure in operation. It is in achieving the transition from vice to virtue that the problems lie: once established, the structures should prove self-perpetuating. Nonetheless, one is still talking about securing a fundamental paradigm shift within the profession.

For this to happen, two preconditions must be met. Firstly, a broader conceptual framework of social work is required in order that the role of research within social work may be defined. What are its strengths and limitations? How far can research determine ends as well as means? What priority should be given to research when findings conflict with other necessary influences on decisions, such as participants' wishes? In the past, social work has been content to allow research to point to the existence of social problems, while denying it any part in the search for solutions. Until there is a broader consensus on the role of social work, it is inevitable that there will be disagreement as to the place of research.

The second condition is more emotional than intellectual. Throughout its history, social work has been obliged to confront apparently ineradicable social problems with limited resources. It has thus tended to value passion and effort above evaluation. Rose-tinted spectacles have often been necessary to sustain the degree of commitment required to plough on where others have long given up. Above all, social workers have had to act, and knowledge, as Nietszche famously observed, is all too frequently the enemy of action. It is hardly surprising that social work has been distinctive in the extent to which its institutions have consistently been overpowered by its charismatics.

There are many drawbacks to what Weber might identify as a charismatic style of leadership, but it undoubtedly engenders a degree of commitment and inspiration which a rational-legal style finds it difficult to match. The solution is to marry the enthusiasm supplied by the heart to the performance that can be achieved by the head. This is easier said than done but the experiments described in this Chapter seem to offer a way forward.

# IO   Lessons learned from first steps

This book has been about the relationship between social research and practice. Volumes have been written about social research in relation to *policy making* and there is much agonising about the connection between *training* and practice. Some commentators have discussed the relationship between policy and practice and the anxiety that social work may be drowning in the swell of government procedure, but the territory described in these pages has remained largely unexplored by others.

It worries us, as it worried some who read our early drafts, that so much here should have been based on the experience of a single research unit working in a narrow field. It may still be objected that the whole exercise is far too self regarding– although we would protest that we have simply sketched the scene for others to elaborate. The truth is that as far as *evaluated* development work in the social care field is concerned, there is little continuous activity to choose. By offering up our own material for dissection we are at least able to make a lasting record of suspect examples in need of improvement.

The first step was to chart the position of research evidence in relation to social work practice, to explain why the star of research has risen and to suggest a proper place for it in a firmament dominated by legal and moral concerns, practical constraints and consumer expectations. Even the most forthright advocate of evidence will surely conclude having read Chapter Two that the need now is not for *more* research but for research better tuned to practitioner requirements.

The tendency among researchers used to be to treat practice as a *tabula rasa* in which to inscribe the wisdom of their evidence. The reality is very different: practitioners commonly regard research and its trappings as a threat or an irrelevance or both, and it is not difficult to see why, considering what it must be like for a social worker to be asked to turn his or her mind from a critical decision on behalf of a child to a scientific development project designed to give a verdict on the cosmetic appearance of yet more paperwork. Indeed, it is surprising that so many professionals are prepared to tolerate and in some cases will even encourage research interference.

The trouble is that there is no structural basis for the relationship between research and practice. Too much turns on the quality of the human relationship and the mutual confidence that exists

The dissemination of research still depends greatly on the 40 minute lecture delivered at a conference organised for professionals. It is a labour intensive approach to the task and, as the Midlands County experiment demonstrates, reaps limited rewards in terms of the transmission of research facts and ideas. But it has important spin-offs: if the 40 minute presentation is good enough to engage an audience and is followed by 20 minutes of sharp questions, it exposes the researcher to the reasonable objections of professionals and drives forward his or her thinking. The public arena can also be a source of the vital trust social services directors are on occasion prepared to invest in research.

Among the many gaps in this book one is extremely significant. There is hardly a word about university and college training. The diagram in Chapter Eight was a reminder that research has little influence on intensive training which in turn has considerable influence on practice. But what about pre-qualification training? Only a handful of universities regularly invite external career researchers to speak on the social work courses and few use evidence to underpin their curriculum. It is an area of work that is only just beginning to be understood. The recently published work by Marsh, P. and Triseliotis, J., *Ready to Practise? Social workers and probation officers–their training and first year in work*, Avebury, 1996, represents a major development.

between enthusiasts. Those directors of social services who recognise the importance of evidence to the future of their profession welcome to their authorities researchers they have come to know and trust. Similarly, from the point of view of research, the success of any enterprise depends greatly on a researcher's determination to understand local conditions and his or her sensitivity to practitioner needs and anxieties. The science of the approach continues to be influenced by the uncertain quality of these personal affections.

We have dealt extensively with the testing of Dartington's *Going Home* materials, which attempt to apply ideas about the separation and return to the general population of looked after children. At first glance, to the untrained eye, the approach might seem to have resembled a medical trial. But there are very wide variations between and within local authorities in the patterns of care and accommodation and these differences reflect not only socio-demography but the traditions, ethos, foibles and much else besides that exist in each administrative location. The consequence is that introducing development materials to the practice of social work professionals is not at all the equivalent of introducing a new medical technique to improve the chances of a patient surviving a disease: not only is the pathology of an illness likely to be more predictable, so is the health professional's response, in particular his or her willingness to accept the value of medical evidence.

If local conditions are to be properly taken into account in future development work, a realistic assessment needs to be made of what social workers know about research. Their knowledge has

been found to be variable, to say the least. The less charitable would say that most social workers know little about the evidence in the Department of Health 'Pink' and 'Blue' Books, even less about the guidance associated with the *Children Act, 1989*. It is certainly the case that before the *Going Home* experiments were inflicted on them, many social workers in Midlands County thought that fewer than half separated children eventually returned to live with relatives. It emerged that only a handful regularly consulted the *Children Act* guidance or were familiar with the research that underpinned it. No wonder the implementation of the Act has sometimes been flawed or that outcomes improved as a result of their contact with the project.

In the absence of any overarching theory of social work with children in need or universal grasp of the precepts of the *Children Act, 1989*, the professional culture of social work is maintained by verbal exchange. Decisions are validated by a consensus of personal experience and understanding and the approach to casework consequently may differ from place to place according to the prevailing sub-culture.

Extreme as this picture may be, it contrasts markedly with the culture of research, which is dependent on the written word and scientific method, seeks consistency between test sites and goes eagerly in search of a comprehensive theory in its sphere of interest. In social work there is a tendency to dismiss criticism from without as a failure on the part of the critic to understand the social work task; in research, such scrutiny is the engine of progress.

One research unit would not dare to dictate to another how it should behave; neither should it seek to prescribe remedies to social workers. It is a researcher's role to explain the links between research and practice and, in the context of ordinary human relationships, trust that others will seek to make the most of the opportunities presented to them. It sounds simple enough but the right relationship is difficult to establish.

The *Children Act, 1989* is framework legislation which gives considerable scope to managers and social workers to fashion services, but it is frequently regarded as prescriptive by local authorities. Similarly, when professional fretfulness coincides with some more general reflection on the relationship between the state and citizen or between central and local government, the issues become clouded. It is not that there is too much guidance or even that guidance limits professionals' freedom— the problem often seems to be that it is delivered to social workers in such a way that they resist.

This is not to say that social work practice and research cultures are incompatible, but that each must better understand the other's differences. To go further may be thought too partisan—but the argument is clearly implicit in the closing pages that children, families, and the professionals that serve them would benefit were the culture of social work to become more like that of research.

★    ★    ★

Probably the most important finding from the development of *Going Home* is that development projects must be targeted more precisely than Dartington's have been to date. The materials were of some benefit to children who had experienced poor parenting over long periods or who had been one of a large family presided over by a lone mother, but in cases where children whose behaviour problems had outstripped the resources of essentially supportive parents, the checklists were of little use. But had the materials been launched three years ago without first being evaluated to the extent reported here, the intention would have been to apply them willy-nilly to every separated child—patently a waste of effort.

In the case of the *Looking After Children* materials a rather similar uncertainty of aim obscures the choice of threshold at which the records are introduced: currently they can be used in short-stay cases where the benefits may be negligible, but not with children long supported at home who would almost certainly gain a great deal from the monitoring process.

Our knowledge of how otherwise to choose target groups and judge the most useful dose of information is still very incomplete. So, to take another example, viz the 'Blue Book' *Child Protection: Messages from Research*, 20,000 copies were distributed by the Department of Health, an assault that certainly had the effect of conveying to child protection professionals the fact that the research existed. But that is not to say that they know any better what the research says or, indeed, that it much matters if they do not. The important target group were the prime movers in the child protection world who seized the overview, read the studies it summarised and were in a position to set about rebuilding children's services in the light of what had been uncovered. In similar circumstances another time they may be the target readership, and with them in mind the equivalent publication may be designed and constructed differently.

There is a strong case for trying to match development services more carefully to the needs of social work professionals, but none at all for making the use of those services compulsory. On the evidence assembled here it is clear that professionals will use research—and anything else on offer—when they recognise the need for it, but will doggedly resist being told what to do. More can be done to demonstrate the benefits of an evidence-based approach to their work but compulsion is unlikely to help.

If the relationship between research and practice is consequently to be built on trust, not compulsion, then a better understanding of the career of a social work professional is called for. One of the simpler messages to emerge, an echo of what has been frequently found in other studies, is to the effect that the more experienced the social worker the more he or she knows and the more he or she achieves for the client. Young professionals, it seems, are nowadays more likely to use supervision as a source of development but persist in their reluctance to read. Older professionals use research more often and are more likely to seek evidence to underpin their decision making. But older professionals were once young themselves. So what must happen along the way?

Closely observing and imitating older colleagues is an aspect of the early stages of any professional career. Later an interest in the trappings of professional membership may develop, giving way as confidence and experience increase to a more divergent pattern of thinking. As the social work profession is presently constructed, the experienced worker seems more likely to use research when seeking to express an unorthodox, divergent view; as a result there may be differences between what is communicated to the novice and what is retained or reserved for personal practice.

These dimensions of the professional process are visible elsewhere. Working with a team of experienced practitioners, Professor Parsloe used the *Going Home* materials to achieve markedly improved outcomes, but the benefits came only much later and then not from any direct action but as a result of injecting prudent caution into decision making. Millham speaks of similar helpful hesitancy when talking about the links between research and policy. Where policy change is concerned, the delay is anticipated and often quite carefully planned, but in the case of practice there is an expectation of immediate improvement, frequently leading to dismay. Evaluated after six

months, the Southern Rural experiment looked to have been fairly disastrous: practitioners had misunderstood the research and their decision making side-stepped the suggestions made in the development materials. Twelve months on, the results were some of the best described here.

What then did Phyllida Parsloe bring to the proceedings? Most of the consequences were unforeseen and largely unintended, so it was hardly a case of bringing the best out of the volunteering professionals and the materials or skilfully hiding their deficiencies. More likely her success was a measure of the level of trust between research and practice she was able to engineer. As a result of her presence the engagement may have been something more meaningful to the social workers than a form-filling exercise. The rapport she established was unusual: just as often the vanities and intellectual snobberies that are still too typical of certain aspects of British university life, provoke justified suspicion and resentment among social services staff.

Inside large organisations like social services departments, the transmission of information touches many minds and the ebb and flow through formal and informal channels is difficult to predict. In Midlands County, for example, the providers of residential care—the least qualified people in the department—were the main conductors of research findings between one half of the county and the other. Understanding how the personal social services are organised has itself become a research priority and may also become a salient consideration among those developing research.

Millham, S. *A Rich Embarrassment or an Embarrassment of Riches?* Dartington Social Research Unit, 1992

# I I  Some rules of thumb

This book does not purport to show others how to do scientific development work on the basis of the Dartington Unit's very limited experience. However, rules for good scientific development work are beginning to emerge and will one day be an accepted part of good research practice. These suggestions simply represent a first attempt to set something down.

▶ the background

1   Development work should be based on an externally reviewed research study which meets accepted standards of excellence.

So, *Looking After Children* requires professionals to link information concerning different aspects of a child's development from one moment to another; *Going Home* is built round the ideas of process and career explored in the scientific study; *Matching Needs and Services* seeks to co-ordinate the planning of children's services so that professionals ask first what does a child need rather than what service has he or she previously received.

2   The theory of the development work should sustain the theory of the research it seeks to take forward; development materials should have the capacity to convey ideas as well as information and to reinvigorate the research.

So, the decision of a professional who ticks all the boxes in a *Going Home* checklist indicating a likely successful reunion, but on **moral** grounds does not allow the child to return should be applauded.

3   A development project should be modest in its intention, taking into account the peripheral role evidence has in the past played in professional decision making.

4   The context for development work is evidence-based social work–the practice of a range of professionals grounded in sound knowledge about the needs of children and families and informed by the best evidence on what is effective.

An important distinction here is between evidence-based social work in which theories of research come to underpin social work practice, and social work which accepts evidence from robust evaluations of services as providing the rationale for intervention. It is in the former that concepts of need, threshold, service and outcome so central to the process of refocusing children's services are linked. The scientific development work described in this book would have little or no value to those who consider there is an alternative theoretical basis for social work.

**5** A considerable amount of remodelling will normally be necessary to convert research findings into usable development materials.

**6** The ability to re-model information is a specialism seldom found in research units. The work may therefore require staff to be employed who have no prior acquaintance with research or practice.

**7** It is important to ensure that the products of development work accurately reflect the scepticism of good research.

**8** Caution must be exercised, too, by the researcher who takes development work into the world of practice and the practitioner who is asked to test it.

**9** The relationship between research and practice with respect to scientific development should be collaborative. Useful comparisions may be made with the professional partnerships of architects and engineers where aesthetic and scientific traditions are combined.

**10** Researchers need to be encouraged to adjust their way of working if the relationship between research and practice described in this book is to be made sustainable.

**11** If it is to be the role of a research unit to test scientific development work, some other organisation will be required to sell the validated product.

Remodelling may be a relatively simple matter of producing an acceptable summary of a 200-page book which links ideas, concepts and facts. Or it may involve making a series of fine judgments about the needs of different users and readers. Factors which statistical analysis may have shown to be insignificant—for example that contact during separation has ceased to be a useful predictor of reunion—may nevertheless be a necessary component of development materials if practitioners are not to be misled by their more general complexion. The territory of remodelling encompasses writing, design, research and information technology.

Designers bring to the world of research and practice knowledge from another critical tradition in which the central tension has been between 'beauty' and 'utility', but a new generation of information designer, born out of the clutter of the information age, is as interested as the researcher in analysis, clarity and objectivity.

The purpose of scientific development work is to put research ideas and facts to a practical test. By its very nature, the message being conveyed will be untried in work with children and families. The researcher must not, therefore, be tempted to sell a product; nor should the practitioner expect development materials to provide simple remedies.

Whatever model is borrowed, the key element is the combination of many skills in the creation of one structure. It is interesting to speculate on the strength of the analogy with architecture: to what extent may a building be said to be a test of architecture?

The application of research by these means places additional burdens both on social work researchers—who must continue to be involved with a study long after it has been published—and practitioners who may be expected to alter their professional behaviour or, where experimental designs are concerned, may find that the latest evidence is not available.

The Department of Health has taken a lead in this, for example, by commissioning and promoting the 'Pink' and 'Blue' Books. There may also be a place for professional organisations such as the British Association of Social Workers the Association of Directors of Social Services or dissemination enterprises such as Research in Practice.

**12** Robust evaluation of scientific development materials requires a number of tests on a number of levels, each relying on different methods.

Testing the products described in this book has focused on use (do professionals find them helpful?), knowledge (having used them do people know more?) and outcomes (do they improve the welfare of vulnerable children and families?). Each test requires different methods. The evaluation of outcome requires more robust experiment than was possible in the case of the *Going Home* materials.

**13** Where experimental designs are concerned, there is considerable risk of generating Hawthorne-type effects. Dartington's approach to date has not adequately tested for them.

There are a number of familiar threats to the usefulness of an experiment. Best known among social researchers are **Hawthorne** effects, where the subjects make special efforts to live up to the expectations of the researcher. At the other extreme are **Sabotage** effects where subjects deliberately behave contrary to expectations and **Placebo** effects where they behave as if the idea being tested were true.

**14** A well-designed development project properly tested will generate new research findings.

So, the first phase of developments from *Going Home* has resulted in a revised publication concerning patterns of separation and return as well as comparisons between the experiences of children looked after before and since the introduction of the *Children Act*, 1989. *Matching Needs and Services* has provided, for the first time, information on the characteristics of all children referred to social service departments.

**15** Elaborateness is not necessarily an indication of good design, rigorous testing or originality.

There is an expectation that designated research centres will produce work at the cutting edge of their field. This pressure tends to generate over-complexity and a compulsion to move on without necessarily consolidating the findings of previous work. There is a tendency, too, to extend development work too far, for example, by designing for the Internet work that wants only a single A4 page, or to make great play of grand new initiatives while neglecting to distribute simple research summaries to the audience one is addressing.

# Endpiece

The Dartington Unit's early attempts to improve the links between research and practice are part of an evolving programme in which scientific development work occupies as much as a third of the entire research programme. *Looking After Children* is in the process of being further tested to gauge its usefulness to local authorities who need to aggregate data for planning purposes, and, as this book goes to press, a development of the Unit's *Making Residential Care Work: Structure and Culture in Children's Homes* study is taking shape. A continuing investigation into risk and protective factors in child care still promises to generate materials which should help practitioners to predict outcomes in individual cases. For the moment at least research and scientific development at Dartington have become closely entwined.

Here and elsewhere, other self-contained projects are emerging. The Centre for Evidence Based Social Services at Exeter University has its sights set on the application of existing research to the personal social services. The Exeter initiative arose out of the Department of Health review *A Wider Strategy for Research and Development Relating to the Personal Social Services* and is equivalent to similar new ventures in health, for example the Cochrane Centre in Oxford and the NHS Centre for Reviews and Dissemination at York. Then there are organisations like Research in Practice and the Family Support Network which are more focused on children's issues and much of whose effort is supported by local authorities. Devon social services have taken the link between research and practice forward another step by sowing the seeds of a social services equivalent of a teaching hospital in the Teignbridge district and commissioning research support from the Dartington Unit.

The context in which all these projects are evolving is changing rapidly—in the case of the technology so rapidly that choosing the right medium for a dissemination exercise is becoming increasingly difficult. In 1993, for example, Dartington's publisher, John Irwin, hinted at the then approaching wonders of publication by CD-ROM; by 1996, just as CD-ROM production was becoming an economic proposition for a Unit of Dartington's size, the spread of the Internet and the arrival of World Wide Web publishing seemed to be about to rid the world of any medium as tangible as compact disc. But in 1997, the frailties of the Internet technologies are temporarily, at least, very apparent… So it goes.

Perhaps not as quickly, but social work is changing too. Most professionals agree there is a need for a common conceptual framework. Most see a place for evidence in whatever framework should emerge. Some go as far as to recognise the theoretical connections between social work research and social work practice which make up the recipe for evidence based social work as it has been described in these pages. But professionals cannot be expected to behave in a way prescribed by research, and researchers fear their work may be derailed by the utilitarian demands of social services departments, for example in the evaluation of schemes based on standardised methods. There is a balance to be struck, but the necessary dialogue is only just beginning.

Furthermore, these issues are unlikely to be as significant for very long. It is as well to remember that thirty years ago, at Seebohm's then fashionable bidding, local authorities were funding the work of 300 social services researchers, but all was soon swept away. How **Tilda Goldberg**, then a major

authority in research, would have revelled in the present discussions about evidence-based social work and the benefits or otherwise of randomised controlled trials. If scientific development work is now to prosper, it must anchor its gains and find ways to maintain the progress it has made during the last decade.

For researchers, scientific development can only ever be a secondary aspect of a greater endeavour. Research and development projects both rely on the best and latest knowledge, but, in the absence of research, development work cannot exist at all. Meanwhile, huge gaps remain in our understanding of family dynamics and children in need: even as the new genetics is revolutionising a taxonomy of disease that has served medicine for over fifty years, social work research is still struggling towards a first rough draft of an equivalent taxonomy of need. The greater challenge is to maintain the momentum of new knowledge that will bring a young research science to maturity.

See for example:
Goldberg, E. M. and Connelly, N. *Evaluative Research in Social Care*, Heinemann, London, 1981 and Goldberg, E.M. and Hatch, S. *A New Look at the Personal Social Services*, Policy Studies Institute, London, 1981

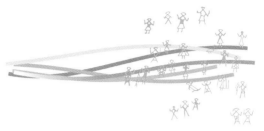

dartington social research series

This book is one of a series dealing with aspects of what is beginning to be known as a common language for the personal social services. The aims is to build up knowledge about different groups of children in need in a form that will be readily understood by policy makers, professionals, researchers and consumers and so make it possible to predict outcomes for such children and to design an effective agency response.

RESEARCH IN PRACTICE concentrates on the connections between the scientific language of researchers, the communication skills of information designers and the demands of practitioners for a clear exposition of the evidence on which their work is based. It introduces the idea of scientific developmen work, a method of applying existing findings in practice which in turn generates new evidence for research. It reinforces the obligations of research developers to evaluate their work and sets a framework for improving understanding.

The language of the personal social services is evolving. It is making use of the results from Dartington studies, of practical developments properly evaluated in a number of test sites and other findings from other groups working in the area. Comment from those making policy, managing services, working directly with children and families or receiving help from personal social service agencies is always welcome. There is a website describing the evolution of the common language at **www.dsru.co.uk** and a series of related papers is available from the Dartington Unit at Warren House, Warren Lane, Dartington, Totnes, Devon, TQ9 6EG email **unit@dsru.co.uk** and Fax +44-1803-866783.